from
COMET
to
CALEDONIA

from COMET *to* CALEDONIA

By DONALD WATSON

A selection of 30 paddle steamer arrangement drawings,
from the 1812 COMET to the 1934 CALEDONIA, including
the INDUSTRY, EDINBURGH CASTLE, IONA,
and the famous JEANIE DEANS.

Specially prepared to illustrate the changes
made to each vessel over it's lifetime, showing each ship as built,
and as it appeared towards the end of it's working life.

First Edition - 1999

ISBN 0 85174 671 3

from
COMET

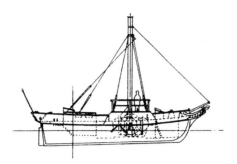

to

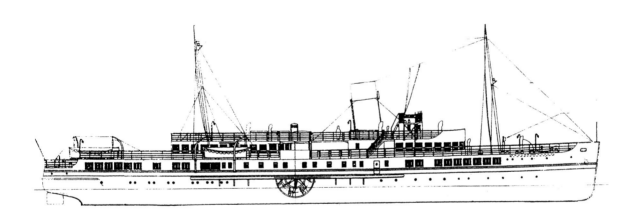

CALEDONIA

By DONALD WATSON

**GENERAL ARRANGEMENT DRAWINGS OF
30 CLYDE RIVER PADDLE STEAMERS
FROM 1812 TO 1934**

CONTENTS

Introduction

Section 1

Paddle Steamer Arrangement Drawings

Section 2

Paddle Steamer Sets

Paddle Steamers with the same name

Acknowledgements and Bibliography

Steamer Index

INTRODUCTION

IT is only rarely that I pay a visit to the City of Glasgow, and it was while on one of these visits that my fascination for Clyde paddle steamers was accidentally started. In a shop one day I picked up a book about Clyde paddle steamers, and after glancing through it, put it down, but on the way out I bought it. That started me off, and I soon found myself looking about for other books on the same subject.

The old pictures of Clyde paddle steamers from pre-war days were awakening some early childhood memories. While I was still only a small boy we had lived in a flat on the sea front at Helensburgh, and it was snatches of memories from those days that kept popping up.

I decided to make a list of Clyde paddle steamers. I began listing all the steamers from about 1900, but soon realised that this would miss out many famous ships, so I decided to go back to the beginning, i.e. 1812, and start from there.

My collection of steamer books grew, and I became a member of the Clyde River Steamer Club, which gave me access to even more steamer information.

I have found, however, that many publications about steamers carry information on sailing times and routes, and only to a lesser extent about the steamers themselves. I am interested in what the ships looked like, how many funnels, how many masts, what changes were made during their lives, and I have found that details of the appearance of many vessels can be rather scarce.

At one time I had considered making small models of some of the early Clyde paddle steamers, but soon discovered that the lack of information made this almost impossible. I decided therefore, that first of all it would be necessary to draw plans of any steamer that I wanted to model.

This entailed gathering and studying all the information and photographs I could find, which has occupied a great deal of my time ever since. The drawing of steamer plans has now become my main interest.

When choosing which paddle steamers I was going to prepare drawings for I decided to try and include some data about all the steamers which carried the same name, where there was enough information to do this.

This book then is the result, and reproduces the 30 plans that I have so far prepared. It must be understood that in the absence of original details about many of these vessels some assumptions and guesswork are necessary in order to produce these drawings, but, to the best of my knowledge, these drawings show the steamers as originally built, and in their final condition after various changes which were made to them.

SECTION 1

PADDLE STEAMER ARRANGEMENT DRAWINGS

Section 1
Paddle Steamer Arrangement Drawings

(Listed Alphabetically)   **(Listed by Date)**

Builder:	**John Wood, Port Glasgow.**
Engine:	**Two cylinder side lever, by James Cook.**
Boiler:	**Two, side by side.**
Owner:	**Unknown.**
Captain:	**Captain John Kay.**
Service:	**Glasgow, Largs, Millport, Ardrossan, Irvine.**
End:	**Unknown.**

ACCORDING to Captain James Williamson in his book of 1904, the *Albion* cost £3450 to construct and equip. Reference to the City of Glasgow Mitchell Library, Glasgow Room, Wotherspoon Collection, shows us that the *Albion* of 1816 was an unusual ship in having two funnels which were placed athwartships, i.e. side by side. This was due to her having two boilers which were positioned one on each side of her two cylinder side lever engine.

Another unusual feature of the *Albion* was that she was designed and built with paddle wheels which were adjustable for height, i.e. the dip of the paddle float in the water could be adjusted to suit the load being carried.

In small ships like the early paddle steamers the dip of the paddle floats in the water could vary greatly, depending on the load carried, and it was to overcome this problem that the variable height paddle wheel was incorporated in the design of this steamer.

Whether this feature proved a success or not is unknown, but as most steamers of the time appear to have fixed paddle shafts, it could be assumed that any benefits gained were far outweighed by the additional cost and complexity of such a mechanism.

During her service between Glasgow and the Firth of Clyde, the *Albion* on one occasion at Largs, struck some old harbour piles and was badly holed. She was temporarily patched up under the direction of Captain Kay, enabling her to be sailed to Greenock, where she was properly repaired.

How the 1816 *Albion* ended her career is not known, but it is fairly certain that she was scrapped, or had left the Clyde by 1834, as another ship named *Albion* was launched in that year.

RE-CONSTRUCTION SHOWING APPEARANCE OF

P.S. "ALBION"

SCALE 1/100 (0.120" = 1 ft)

BUILT OF WOOD IN 1816
BY
JOHN WOOD Cº
PORT GLASGOW

LENGTH O.A.
LENGTH B.P.   84'-11"
BREADTH (HULL) 16'-1"
BREADTH (EXT.)
DEPTH   10'
DRAUGHT
WEIGHT   68 TONS (GROSS)

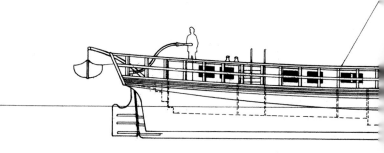

DRAWN BY   D. WATSON
              CLARKSTON
              GLASGOW   SEPT. 1991

BASED ON DATA FROM VARIOUS SOURCES, AND
CONTEMPORARY STEAMER PICTURES.

6" = 50 ft

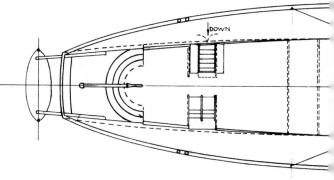

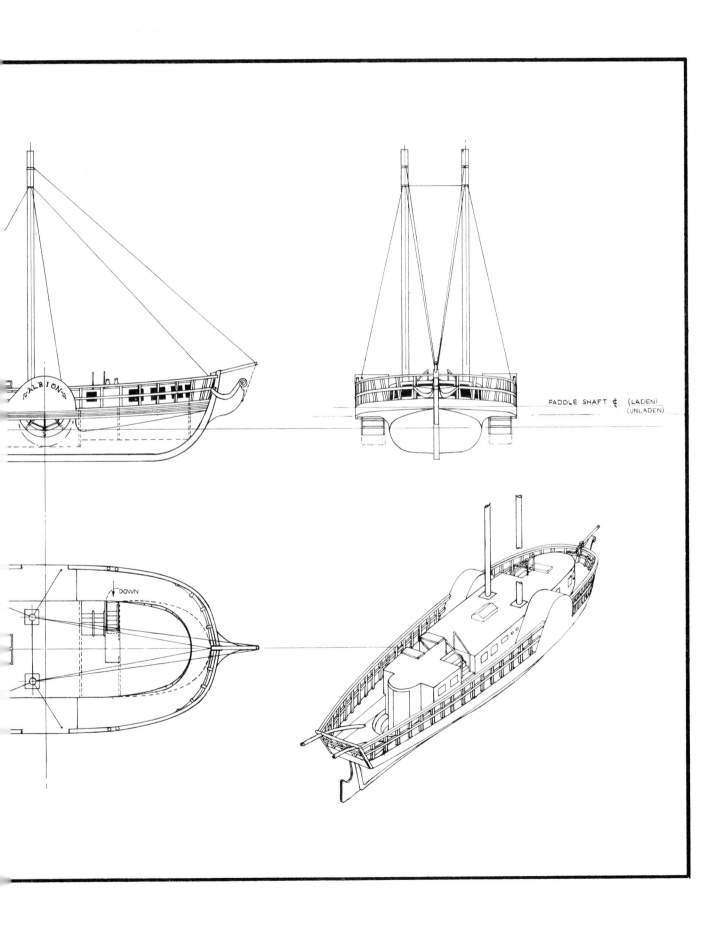

PADDLE SHAFT ℄ (LADEN)
(UNLADEN)

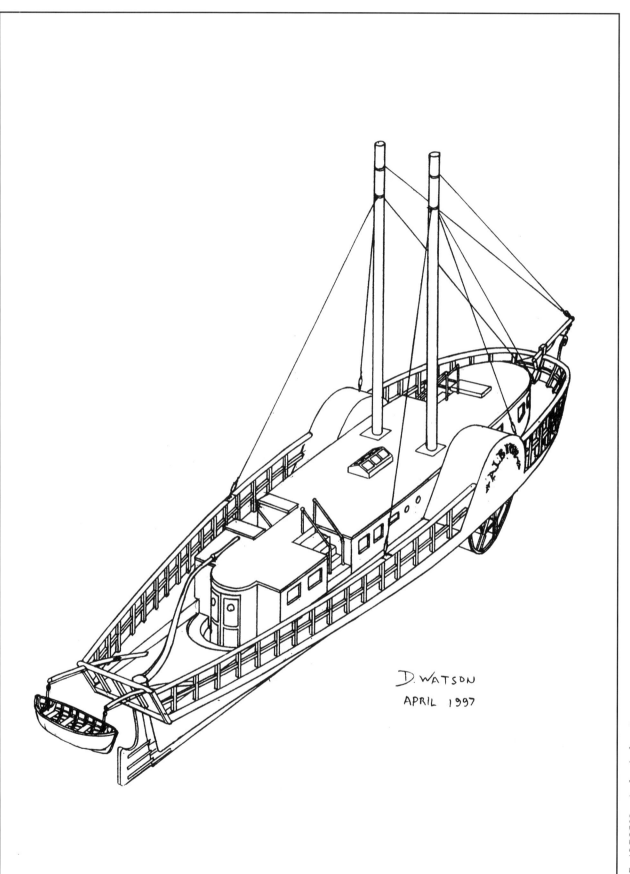

D. WATSON
APRIL 1997

Builder:	**John & Charles Wood, Port Glasgow.**	
Engine:	**Two, side lever, built by the Greenhead Foundry.**	
Boiler:	**Low pressure flue boiler.**	
Owner:	**Unknown.**	**1815-1816**
	Unknown.	**1816-1817**
	James Watt, junior.	**1817-1819**
	Steen Anderson Bille (Denmark).	**1819-1822**
	Lauritz Nikolaj Hvidt (Denmark).	**1822-1843**
	B.U.	**1843**
Captain (1st):	**Captain Leitch.**	
Service:	**Glasgow, Greenock, Rothesay.**	
End:	**Broken up 1843.**	

THIS was the first of six steamers, to carry the name *Caledonia*, which were to be built on the river Clyde. She was the seventh steamer built by John & Charles Wood, was the second to have two engines, and was the largest yet built on the river. She was launched on 27th April, 1815.

The *Caledonia* was built with paddle wheel sponsons which extended for the full length of the hull, which was not an unusual feature at that time, giving an increased deck area. The machinery space was covered and she had cabins positioned at either end of this. Passenger deck area was provided on the cabins and machinery roofs, and on the increased deck space made available by the extended paddle sponsons.

At the aft end of the ship, behind the engine and boiler space, was the first class cabin, which consisted of a best cabin, with, at the fore end, a private ladies cabin and toilet. Access to the first class accommodation was by a short covered companionway positioned at the rear end of the cabin.

A second class accommodation cabin, along with a toilet, the kitchen and the stewards room, was provided in the forward cabin, and access to these areas was obtained by a short covered companionway on the starboard side. The toilet was positioned on the opposite side of the cabin to the companionway, so that these two features separated the kitchen and stewards room from the second class cabin.

On deck, the first and second class areas

Birmingham Central Library Steamboat Box Collection of Boulton & Watt (No. 71)

were separated by a banister, or rail, positioned at the aft end of the machinery space.

The *Caledonia* had a single mast on which a square sail could be set, and she carried the figurehead of a woman. At the stern, which was said to have a lavish gilt decoration, a small rowing boat was carried on outriggers.

Although well fitted out for the comfort of her passengers, the *Caledonia* was apparently not as successful on her Glasgow-Greenock run as her owners might have hoped, and consequently, in July 1816, she was moved to the Thames, sailing down the West coast, round Lands End and through the Channel. She plied between London and Margate, commanded by Edward Phipps. This venture was apparently no more successful than her river Clyde operation, and she was eventually laid up. Whether she had been sold on her transfer to the Thames, or

still had her original owners is not clear.

It is known, however, that James Watt, junior, then a partner in the firm of Boulton, Watt & Co., bought her in April 1817, and by July had supplied the vessel with two new engines and a new boiler.

With James Watt, junior, aboard, and commanded by Captain Wager, the *Caledonia* sailed, in October, from Margate to Rotterdam in the Netherlands. She left Rotterdam later in the month, sailed up the river Rhine to Cologne and Koblenz, and visited Antwerp on the river Schelde before returning to the Thames by January 1818. She is said to have been the first steamboat to sail on the river Rhine.

The experience gained on these voyages resulted in some alterations being made. In 1818, changes were made to the engines, and a new funnel was fitted. Experiments were also carried out with the paddle wheels, which resulted in the original 10.5ft diameter wheels being replaced with wheels of 13ft diameter with eight floats.

After being sold in 1819 to Danish owners, it would appear, judging by old pictures and drawings, that some changes were made to the accommodation arrangements. The first class private ladies cabin seems to have been dispensed with in order to allow the fitting of an additional covered entrance on the starboard side, to the best cabin. Internal changes to the cabins may also have been carried out but what these might have been is not known. It is thought by the writer that these changes were done when the *Caledonia* was used as a royal yacht, as this seems to have happened on occasion.

The *Caledonia* was reboilered in 1821, the new boiler being supplied by Boulton & Watt Co.

The *Caledonia* continued to serve her Danish owners until she was replaced by a new ship in 1830, after which she became the relief ship until eventually broken up in 1843.

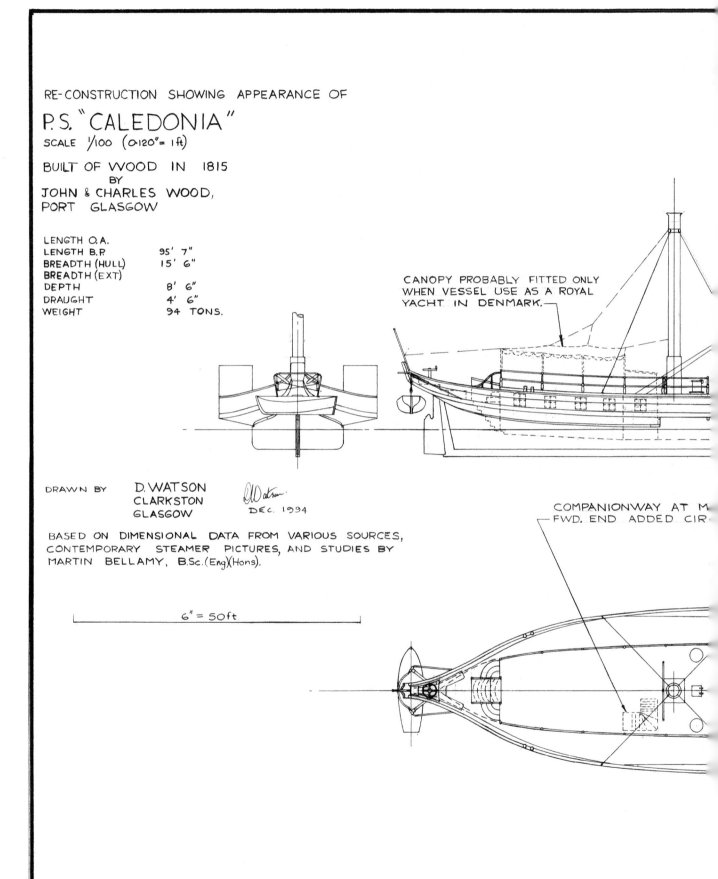

RE-CONSTRUCTION SHOWING APPEARANCE OF

P.S. "CALEDONIA"

SCALE 1/100 (0·120"= 1ft)

BUILT OF WOOD IN 1815
BY
JOHN & CHARLES WOOD,
PORT GLASGOW

LENGTH O.A.	
LENGTH B.P	95' 7"
BREADTH (HULL)	15' 6"
BREADTH (EXT)	
DEPTH	8' 6"
DRAUGHT	4' 6"
WEIGHT	94 TONS.

CANOPY PROBABLY FITTED ONLY
WHEN VESSEL USE AS A ROYAL
YACHT IN DENMARK.

DRAWN BY D. WATSON
CLARKSTON
GLASGOW
DEC. 1994

BASED ON DIMENSIONAL DATA FROM VARIOUS SOURCES,
CONTEMPORARY STEAMER PICTURES, AND STUDIES BY
MARTIN BELLAMY, B.Sc.(Eng)(Hons).

6" = 50ft

COMPANIONWAY AT M
FWD. END ADDED CIR

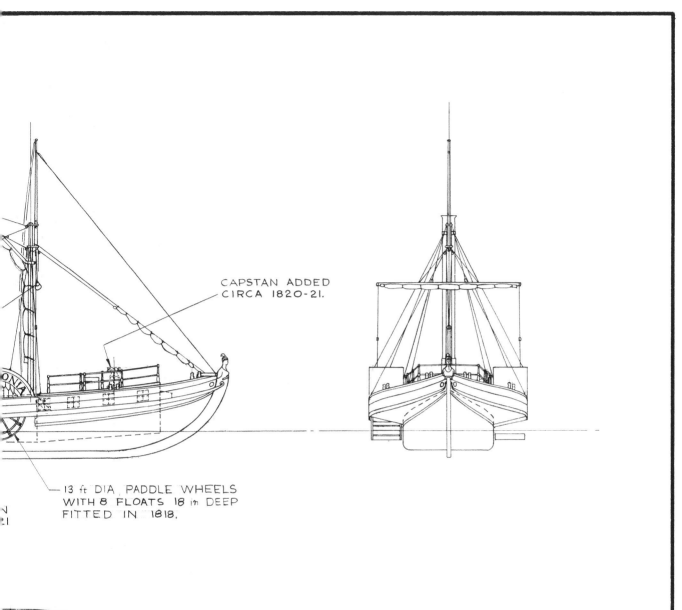

CAPSTAN ADDED
CIRCA 1820-21.

13 ft DIA. PADDLE WHEELS
WITH 8 FLOATS 18 in DEEP
FITTED IN 1818.

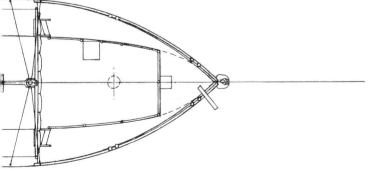

Builder:	**John Reid & Co, Port Glasgow.**
Engine:	**Rankin & Blackmore, Greenock.** **Single crank two cylinder comp. tandem surface condensing.**
Boiler:	**Two navy, or locomotive type.**
Owner:	**Caledonian Stm. Pkt. Co.** **1889-1923** **London Midland & Scottish Rly.** **1923-1933** **B.U. by T. Ward Ltd., Barrow..** **1933**
Captain (1st):	**Captain C. Mitchell.**
Service:	**Glasgow, Gourock, Rothesay & the Holy Loch.**
End:	**Broken up 1933.**

TO own and operate paddle steamers on the river Clyde, connecting with passenger trains to and from Glasgow, was the intention of the Caledonian Railway Company, and to this end orders had been placed for the building of new paddle steamers. Unfortunately for the Company, they had placed the orders in anticipation of obtaining parliamentary approval for their plans, but, due to the objections of other steamer operators, this was not immediately forthcoming.

To overcome this problem, the directors of the Railway Company decided to establish a separate concern, thus on the 8th May, 1889, the Caledonian Steam Packet Company was formed.

The first ship to be completed was named the *Caledonia*. She was launched on the 6th May, 1889, and began service in the following June. Her builder, John Reid of Port Glasgow, was the grand nephew of John Wood, builder of the first Clyde paddle steamer, the *Comet*.

The P.S. *Caledonia* had full width saloons, both fore and aft, with a companionway from the fore deck to the promenade deck at the forward end, and a companionway, aft of the paddles, from the promenade deck to the aft saloon.

She was equipped with engine telegraphs, but in addition was fitted with docking telegraphs fore and aft, so that the master could instruct the crewmen handling the mooring lines without the need for shouting and signaling.

When originally built, her paddle sponsons featured radial vents, and carried an elaborate design featuring a shield bearing a Lion Rampant with a rearing horse on either side, along with an assortment of intricate artwork.

The most unusual feature of the *Caledonia*, however, was that the engine room was no longer closed off from view, but was fitted around with handrails, so that the public could see the engine in operation. The two cylinders, mounted in tandem and operating the big single crank and connecting rods via a common piston rod, must have been a very impressive sight. The boilers of course were not in view, being of the closed stokehold forced draft type. The *Caledonia* was the first Clyde steamer to be equipped with this type of boiler.

Like most steamers of that time, the bridge of the *Caledonia* was positioned amidships, between the paddle boxes, which was behind the forward placed funnel.

Two life boats were carried, mounted aft on the paddle sponsons, but in 1913 this was increased to three, along with the addition of other flotation equipment.

In 1893, as an experiment, the *Caledonia* was modified to burn fuel oil instead of coal, but although successful, this method of fuelling was not proceeded with as the cost of fuel oil became prohibitive.

It may have been about that time that the paddle sponsons were altered, the radial vents being replaced by horizontal slots. As far as can be determined the ornamental work was unchanged.

The *Caledonia* was reboilered in 1903, and at the same time the bridge was repositioned forward of the funnel. The old traditional position for the bridge of a paddle steamer, between the paddle boxes, had for some time been a cause of concern, as it restricted the master's view ahead. Although no lives were lost, the running down by the *Caledonia*, of a small boat carrying holiday makers in July 1889, and the consequent public outcry, no doubt added to the pressure on builders, owners and operators, to make the change.

In 1913, after the *Titanic* disaster, an additional lifeboat was carried, being mounted on the starboard side at the stern, and a deck house was added over the promenade deck aft companionway, with additional flotation gear mounted on top.

The *Caledonia* was requisitioned in 1917, and became auxiliary minesweeper, No. PP557, serving in the English Channel. In 1919 she was used as a transport, and it was while on this service on the river Seine in France that she and a Norwegian ship, the *Kalfond*, collided. The *Caledonia* was badly damaged, but was fully repaired and eventually returned to her old duties on the Clyde in 1920.

After serving for 44 years on the Clyde, sailing to Rothesay and then on the Holy Loch service, the *Caledonia* was eventually sold for breaking up at Barrow in 1933.

The *Caledonia* had two sister ships, both of which were built in 1890. These, the P.S.'s. *Marchioness of Breadalbane*, and *Marchioness of Bute*, were almost identical to the *Caledonia*, but both had the bridge positioned forward of the funnel, and when built, neither had a companionway from promenade deck to the fore deck, although this was added to the *Marchioness of Breadalbane* sometime during the 1914-18 war. The paddle box vents were slightly different also, the *Marchioness's* having seven columns of vents while the *Caledonia* had only six. It is understandable that it is easy to be mistaken when trying to identify these ships in old pictures.

The 1889 P.S. Caledonia, as she appeared prior to 1903.

Reproduced courtesy of Scottish Maritime Museum

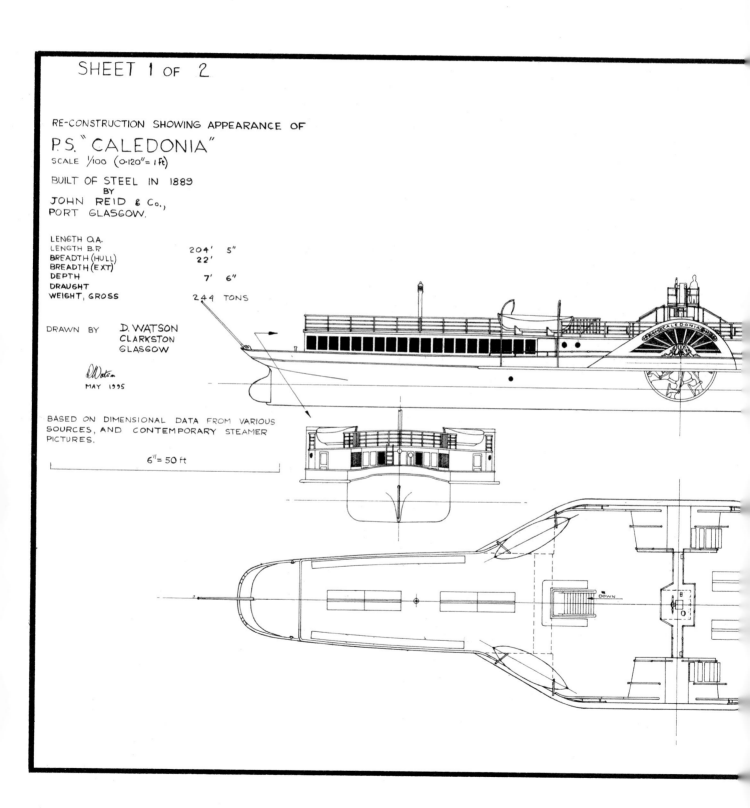

SHEET 1 OF 2

RE-CONSTRUCTION SHOWING APPEARANCE OF

P.S. "CALEDONIA"
SCALE 1/100 (0·120"= 1 ft)

BUILT OF STEEL IN 1889
BY
JOHN REID & Co.,
PORT GLASGOW.

LENGTH O.A.	
LENGTH B.P.	204' 5"
BREADTH (HULL)	22'
BREADTH (EXT)	
DEPTH	7' 6"
DRAUGHT	
WEIGHT, GROSS	244 TONS

DRAWN BY   D. WATSON
             CLARKSTON
             GLASGOW

             D.Watson
MAY 1995

BASED ON DIMENSIONAL DATA FROM VARIOUS
SOURCES, AND CONTEMPORARY STEAMER
PICTURES.

6"= 50 ft

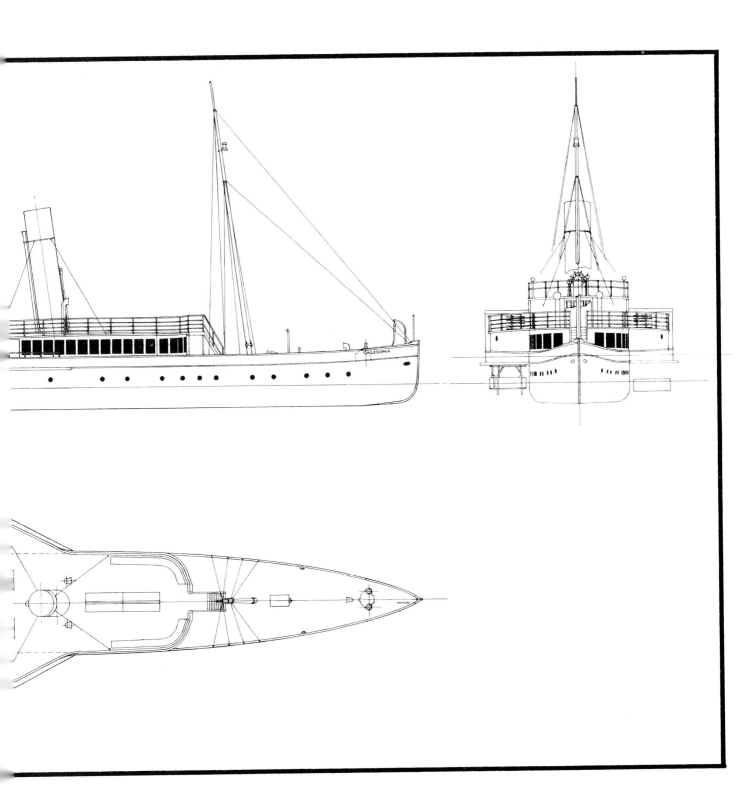

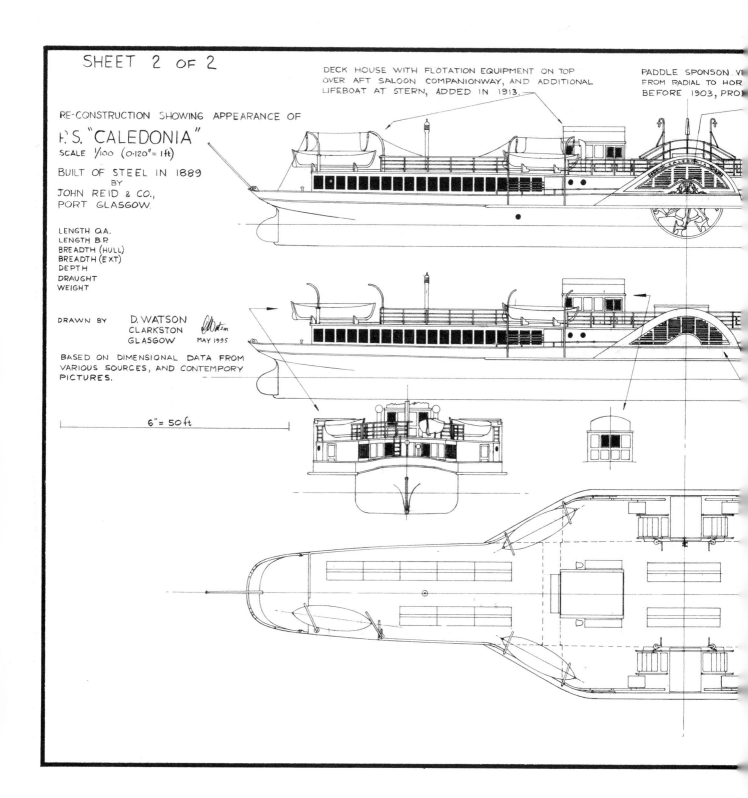

SHEET 2 OF 2

DECK HOUSE WITH FLOTATION EQUIPMENT ON TOP
OVER AFT SALOON COMPANIONWAY, AND ADDITIONAL
LIFEBOAT AT STERN, ADDED IN 1913.

PADDLE SPONSON V
FROM RADIAL TO HOR
BEFORE 1903, PRO

RE-CONSTRUCTION SHOWING APPEARANCE OF

P.S. "CALEDONIA"

SCALE ¹/₁₀₀ (0·120" = 1ft)

BUILT OF STEEL IN 1889
BY
JOHN REID & CO.,
PORT GLASGOW.

LENGTH O.A.
LENGTH B.P.
BREADTH (HULL)
BREADTH (EXT)
DEPTH
DRAUGHT
WEIGHT

DRAWN BY   D. WATSON
            CLARKSTON
            GLASGOW   MAY 1995

BASED ON DIMENSIONAL DATA FROM
VARIOUS SOURCES, AND CONTEMPORY
PICTURES.

6" = 50 ft

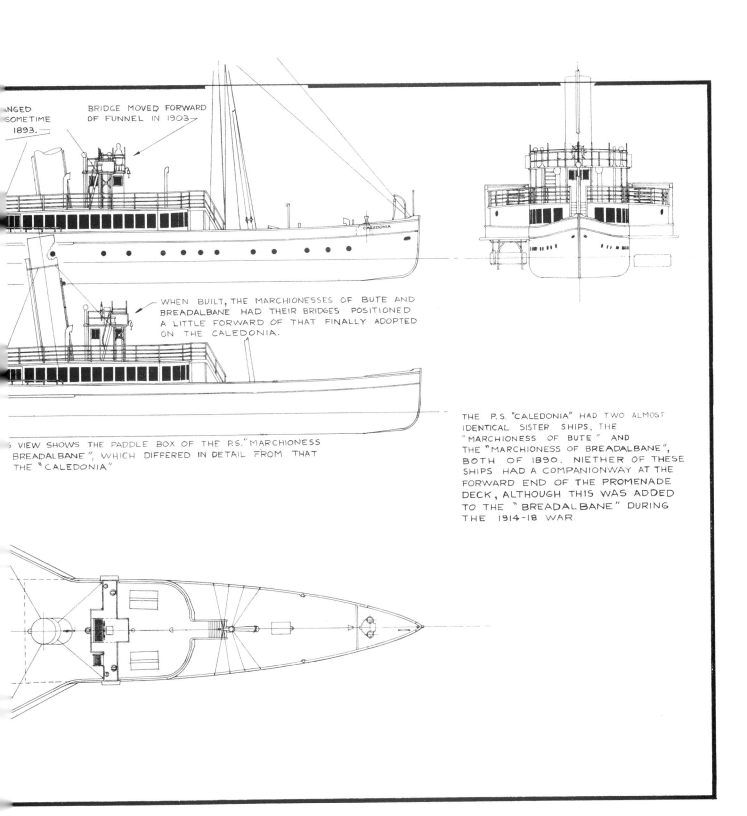

ANGED
SOMETIME
1893.

BRIDGE MOVED FORWARD
OF FUNNEL IN 1903

CALEDONIA

WHEN BUILT, THE MARCHIONESSES OF BUTE AND
BREADALBANE HAD THEIR BRIDGES POSITIONED
A LITTLE FORWARD OF THAT FINALLY ADOPTED
ON THE CALEDONIA.

S VIEW SHOWS THE PADDLE BOX OF THE P.S."MARCHIONESS
BREADALBANE", WHICH DIFFERED IN DETAIL FROM THAT
THE "CALEDONIA"

THE P.S. "CALEDONIA" HAD TWO ALMOST
IDENTICAL SISTER SHIPS, THE
"MARCHIONESS OF BUTE" AND
THE "MARCHIONESS OF BREADALBANE",
BOTH OF 1890. NIETHER OF THESE
SHIPS HAD A COMPANIONWAY AT THE
FORWARD END OF THE PROMENADE
DECK, ALTHOUGH THIS WAS ADDED
TO THE "BREADALBANE" DURING
THE 1914-18 WAR.

Builder:	William Denny & Brothers, Dumbarton. Yard No. 1266.
Engine:	William Denny & Brothers, Dumbarton. Three cylinder triple expansion diagonal. Closed stokehold.
Boiler:	Two cylindrical navy type.

Owner:	Caledonian Steam Packet Co.	1934-1970
	W.H. Arnott Young & Co. Dalmuir.	1970-1972
	Bass Charrington Ltd.	1972-1980

Captain (1st):	Unknown.
Service:	Gourock, Wemyss Bay, Dunoon, Rothesay & the Kyles.
End:	Severely damaged by fire in April 1980, then B.U. near Sittingbourne, Kent.

THE first steamer owned by the Caledonian Steam Packet Co. was withdrawn in 1933, after 44 years service. On the 1st of February in the following year her replacement was launched and was given the same name, that is, *CALEDONIA*. The new *Caledonia* came into service on 31st March.

When the 1934 P.S. *Caledonia* was being designed and built, her design included the ability to carry vehicles, as both her builders and the C.S.P. were aware of the growing number of motor cars and vans coming into use, and recognised the need for transport of these to the various Clyde ports and islands.

The new *Caledonia* did not have the usual rounded sponsons over the paddle wheels, but instead had the line of the ship's hull bulged out to include the paddles, and the deck above widened to accommodate the bulges. This gave a wide and spacious deck area over the paddles, which could be made available for the loading of vehicles such as cars, vans, or caravans. Both forward and aft of this area, deck shelters were located, the roofs of which provided observation decks for passenger use. The forward and aft observation decks were connected by two gangways over the wide vehicle deck area. Both gangways could be raised up, being hinged to the forward observation deck, thus giving clearance for any tall van or caravan that it might be necessary to carry.

The captain's cabin was positioned atop the

forward observation deck, and on top of the cabin was a flying bridge which projected beyond the breadth of the hull, another departure from the normal design.

Other novel features were the cruiser stern, and the single elliptical funnel. The *Caledonia* was equipped with three 21ft lifeboats, and had two masts, a feature which seemed to have lost favour with Clyde steamer owners since the mid 1800's.

She originally had paddle wheels carrying seven floats, but suffered from vibration problems with these, and in March 1937 redesigned wheels with eight slightly smaller floats were fitted.

The *Caledonia* was able to carry 1300 passengers, and although many steamers had come from the Denny yard at Dumbarton, she was the first Denny paddle steamer to serve on the River Clyde since the 1890 *Duchess of Hamilton*.

When war was declared in 1939, the *Caledonia* was commissioned as a minesweeper, and given the name HMS *Goatfell*, pennant No. 125, and served in the eleventh minesweeper flotilla.

Later she became a patrol vessel and flack ship.

It was not until 1945 that she was released and returned to her builders for reconditioning, before again appearing in service on the Clyde in May 1946.

One of the changes made for her service with the Royal Navy, was the erection of an enclosed wheelhouse on the flying bridge. This feature was retained when she was reconditioned by Denny's. Pictures illustrating the *Caledonia* after the war show her to have the stern lifeboat mounted on the starboard side, whereas prior to the war it was on the port side. It is thought that this change was made when replacing the lifeboat during reconditioning, although this has not been absolutely confirmed. Another small but noticeable change resulting from the

reconditioning was the addition of rubbing strakes near the bow, and the extending of the rear strake around the stern.

When she again took up her Clyde duties she was able to carry 1700 passengers.

In 1954-5 the *Caledonia* went to Troon for reboilering with new navy boilers, and the opportunity was taken then to convert her from coal to oil burning.

With the advent of Kingston Bridge the *Caledonia* had her masts shortened in 1969, and in September of that year was the last steamer to call at Bridge Wharf, before it was finally closed.

The *Caledonia* was withdrawn from service in November 1969, making her the second last paddle steamer in the C.S.P. fleet, the very last paddle steamer being the very well known *Waverley*, now the flagship of the Paddle Steamer Preservation Society.

Early in 1970 she was sold to W.H. Arnott Young & Co. Ltd., who took her to their Dalmuir basin and renamed her *OLD CALEDONIA*. She was then sold by them in 1971 to Bass Charrington Ltd., who moved her to the Royal Albert Dock in London for conversion to a floating restaurant and pub. When ready, she was moored by the Victoria Embankment near Waterloo Bridge on the Thames.

The *Caledonia*, or *Old Caledonia*, as she was now called, did no more sailing, but remained a floating hostelry until the 27th of April, 1980, when she was severely damaged by fire. Salvage proved uneconomical, so she was finally scrapped, and went for breaking up at Milton Creek, near Sittingbourne in Kent.

So passed the last paddle steamer named *Caledonia*, although other ships have since carried the name, these have all been of the screw propulsion type.

The engines of the *Caledonia*, however, were saved, and can be seen in a museum in Liphook, Hampshire.

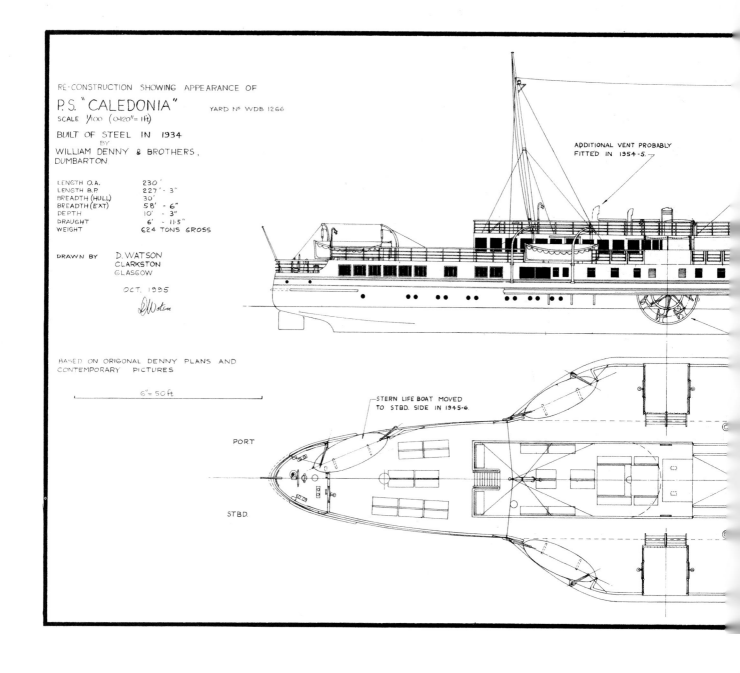

RE-CONSTRUCTION SHOWING APPEARANCE OF

P.S. "CALEDONIA"   YARD Nº WDB 1266
SCALE ¹/₁₀₀ (0·120"= 1 ft)

BUILT OF STEEL IN 1934
BY
WILLIAM DENNY & BROTHERS,
DUMBARTON

LENGTH O.A.   230'
LENGTH B.P.   227' - 3"
BREADTH (HULL)   30'
BREADTH (EXT)   58' - 6"
DEPTH   10' - 3"
DRAUGHT   6' - 11·5"
WEIGHT   624 TONS GROSS

DRAWN BY   D. WATSON
            CLARKSTON
            GLASGOW

            OCT. 1995

BASED ON ORIGONAL DENNY PLANS AND
CONTEMPORARY PICTURES

6"= 50 ft

ADDITIONAL VENT PROBABLY
FITTED IN 1954-5.

STERN LIFE BOAT MOVED
TO STBD. SIDE IN 1945-6.

PORT

STBD.

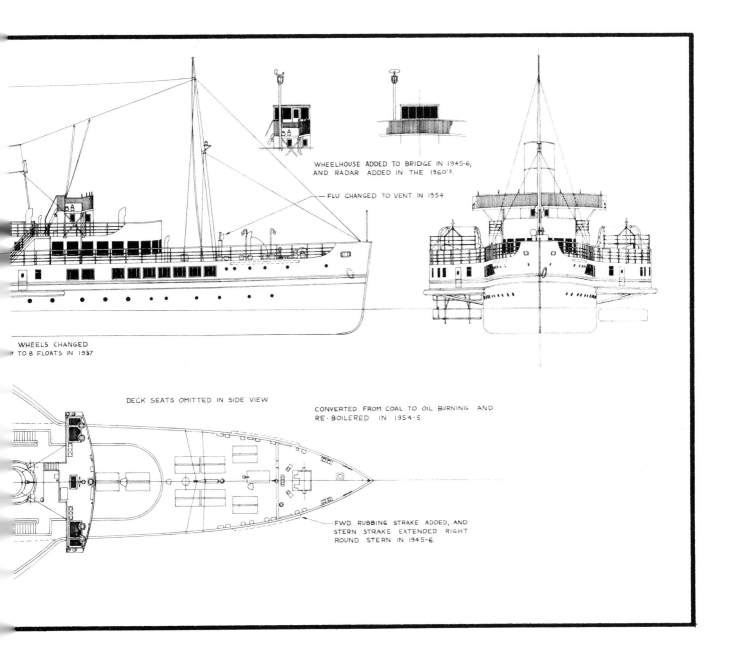

WHEELHOUSE ADDED TO BRIDGE IN 1945-6,
AND RADAR ADDED IN THE 1960'S.

FLU CHANGED TO VENT IN 1954

WHEELS CHANGED
TO 8 FLOATS IN 1937

DECK SEATS OMITTED IN SIDE VIEW

CONVERTED FROM COAL TO OIL BURNING AND
RE-BOILERED IN 1954-5.

FWD. RUBBING STRAKE ADDED, AND
STERN STRAKE EXTENDED RIGHT
ROUND STERN IN 1945-6.

Reproduced courtesy of The Mitchell Library, Glasgow City Libraries & Archives
The 1934 P.S. Caledonia

1853　　　　　　　　　　　　　　　　　　　CHANCELLOR

Builder:	**W. Denny & Bros, Dumbarton.**	
Engine:	**Unknown.**	
Boiler:	**Haystack.**	
Owner:	**Dumbarton Steam Boat Co.**	**1853-1863**
Captain (1st):	**John Wilson.**	
Service:	**Glasgow – Arrochar.**	
End:	**Sold to Confederate States 1863.**	

THE 1853 *Chancellor* was the first of three ships of that name to serve on the Glasgow – Arrochar route (the second and third being built in 1864 and 1890 respectively).

She served on the route until sold by her owners in 1863 to the Confederate States of America for blockade running during the American Civil War.

During the winter "off season" the *Chancellor* was laid up, along with many other steamers, at Bowling Harbour.

In 1856 exceptional gales wreaked havoc at Bowling, causing damage to many ships, and driving the *Chancellor* on to the harbour breakwater. The damage was repaired and the *Chancellor* was back on station when the summer season opened up.

Reproduced courtesy of The Mitchell Library, Glasgow City Libraries & Archives
The 1853 Chancellor　　　　　　　23

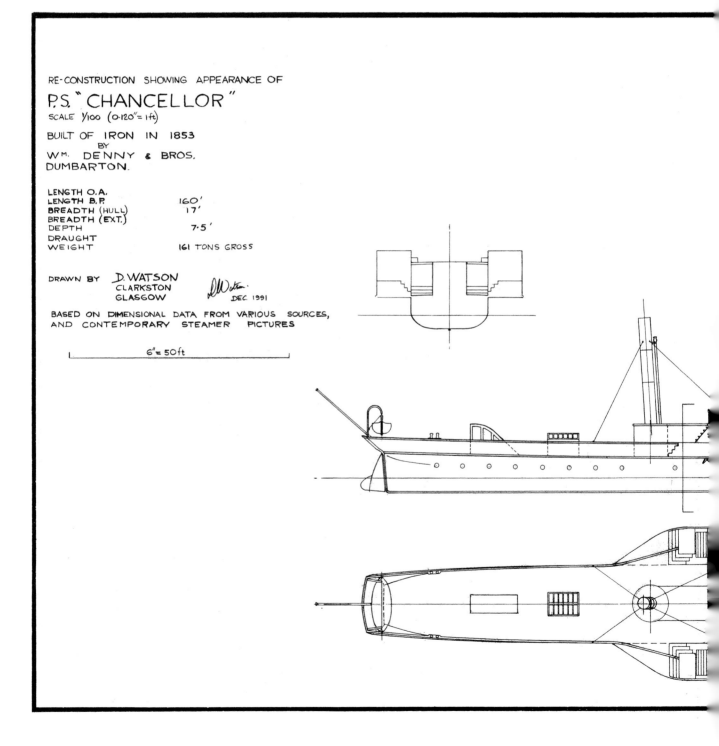

RE-CONSTRUCTION SHOWING APPEARANCE OF

P.S. "CHANCELLOR"

SCALE 1/100 (0·120"= 1ft)

BUILT OF IRON IN 1853
BY
Wᴹ. DENNY & BROS.
DUMBARTON.

LENGTH O.A.
LENGTH B.P.   160'
BREADTH (HULL)   17'
BREADTH (EXT.)
DEPTH   7·5'
DRAUGHT
WEIGHT   161 TONS GROSS

DRAWN BY   D. WATSON
           CLARKSTON
           GLASGOW   DEC. 1991

BASED ON DIMENSIONAL DATA FROM VARIOUS SOURCES,
AND CONTEMPORARY STEAMER PICTURES

6"= 50ft

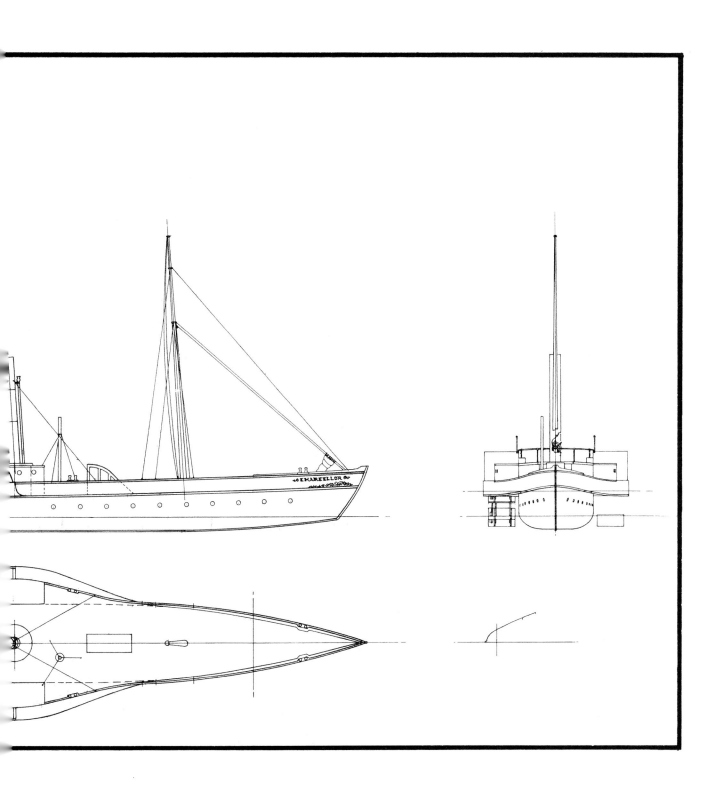

1864-1880	CHANCELLOR
1880-1893	Re-named SHANDON
1893-1895	Re-named DANIEL ADAMSON

Builder:	**Blackwood & Gordon, Port Glasgow.**
Engine:	**Blackwood & Gordon, Port Glasgow.**
Boiler:	**Haystack.**

Owner:		
	Loch Long & Loch Lomond Stm. Boat Co.	**1864-1880**
	Keith & Campbell.	**1880-1884** (Shandon)
	W. Buchanan.	**1884-1888**
	A. Smallet.	**1888-1893**
	Ship Canal Pass. Stmr. Co. (1893) Ltd. Manchester	**1893-1895** (Daniel Adamson)
	James Orr	**1895-1896 - B.U.**

Captain (1st):	**Mr Neilson.**
Service:	**Glasgow – Dumbarton – Helensburgh – Arrocher.**
End:	**Broken up 1896.**

THE 1864 PS *Chancellor* was the second of three ships of that name to serve on the Glasgow – Arrocher route, (the first and third being built in 1853 and 1880 respectively).

The *Chancellor* (1864) was of unusual design in having the paddle wheel sponsons extended for the full length of the hull, from stem to stern, which provided a large deck area. Although unusual for steamers of this date, the design was in fact fairly common during the early years of Clyde steamer development. The PS *Elizabeth* 1812, *Industry* 1813, *Clyde* 1813, *Duke of Argyle* 1814, and *Albion* 1816, for example, being of this type.

Originally, *Chancellor* had no mast but about 1881, while sailing for Keith & Campbell, a foremast was added, presumably to enable a light to be carried.

At the official opening in 1875 of the new Dumbarton pier built out from Castle Rock, *Chancellor* of 1864, was one of the attendant steamers taking part in the ceremony.

In 1884 this ship, now renamed *Shandon*, gave a trial service from Paisley Harbour to Rothesay, and again in 1891 Paisley Harbour was the starting point for a trial sail to the Gareloch.

Reproduced courtesy of The Mitchell Library, Glasgow City Libraries & Archives
The 1864 Chancellor

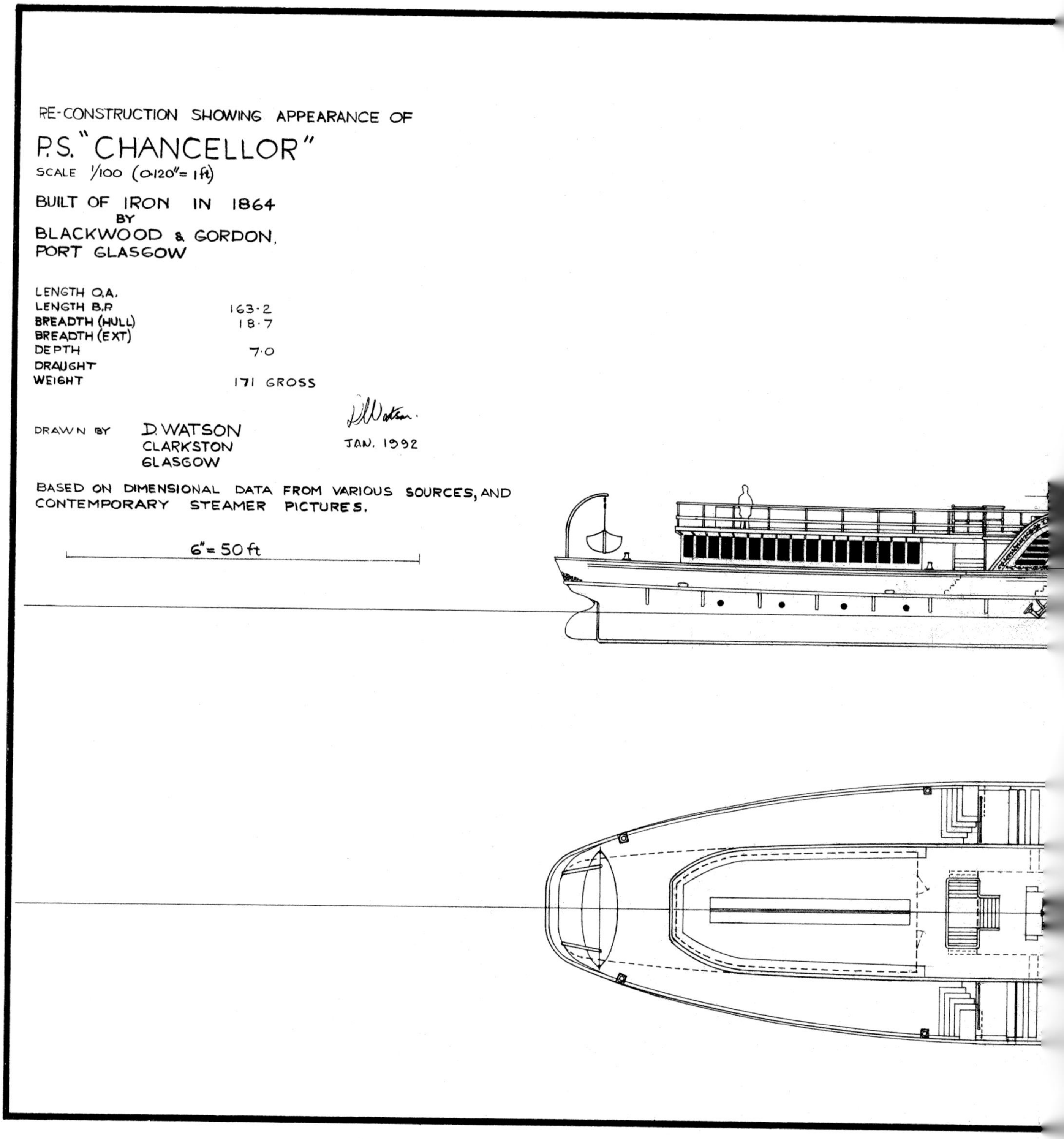

RE-CONSTRUCTION SHOWING APPEARANCE OF

P.S. "CHANCELLOR"

SCALE 1/100 (0·120" = 1ft)

BUILT OF IRON IN 1864
                    BY
BLACKWOOD & GORDON,
PORT GLASGOW

LENGTH O.A.	
LENGTH B.P.	163·2
BREADTH (HULL)	18·7
BREADTH (EXT)	
DEPTH	7·0
DRAUGHT	
WEIGHT	171 GROSS

DRAWN BY   D. WATSON
            CLARKSTON   JAN. 1992
            GLASGOW

BASED ON DIMENSIONAL DATA FROM VARIOUS SOURCES, AND
CONTEMPORARY STEAMER PICTURES.

6" = 50 ft

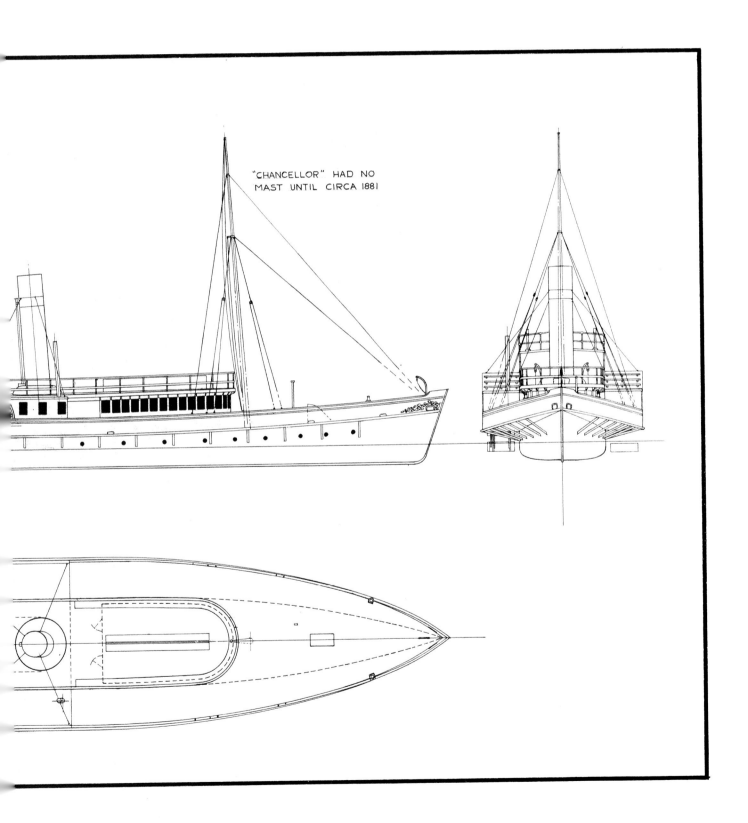

"CHANCELLOR" HAD NO
MAST UNTIL CIRCA 1881

Builder:	Robert Chambers, Dumbarton.	
Engine:	Mathew Paul & Co.	
Boiler:	Haystack.	
Owner:	Loch Long & Loch Lomond Steam Bt. Co.	1880-1885
	Loch Goil & Loch Long Steam Bt. Co.	1885-1891
	Glasgow & South Western Railway.	1891-1901
	La Herculina Ferrolana, Spain.	1901-1919
Captain (1st):	T. Nelson.	
Service:	Helensburgh, Arrochar.	
End:	Broken up 1919.	

LIKE her two predecessors of the same name, the 1880 PS *Chancellor* served on the Helensburgh/Arrochar route. She was the last paddle steamer of that name to be built for Clyde service, and all in all, plied for 21 years on the River Clyde for her various owners.

She was built in Dumbarton in the same shipyard that, twelve years before, had seen the building of the famous clipper ship *Cutty Sark* by The Scott Linton Company. Built of steel, the *Chancellor* was the third Clyde steamer to use this material, the first and second being the PS *Windsor Castle* of 1859, and David McBrayne's PS *Columba* of 1878, respectively.

Her engines were open to view by the passengers, a feature which became common practice on Clyde paddle steamers. She was provided with deck saloons, fore and aft, with narrow alleyways all round, and was in fact the last Clyde service steamer built in this way. Subsequent ships were fitted with full width deck saloons.

Below the main deck, the accommodation had only limited headroom, which was not uncommon in river steamers of that time.

The *Chancellor* was not regarded as a fast ship, her average speed being about 14 knots. In 1892, after having her haystack boiler replaced by a navy type boiler, and having her simple diagonal engine converted to a compound diagonal, her average speed was increased to 15 knots.

When built she had sponson houses in front of the paddle boxes, but aft of the paddle boxes the deck was open. Sponson houses were added aft of the paddle boxes during her overhaul in 1892.

Reproduced courtesy of The Mitchell Library, Glasgow City Libraries & Archives

The 1880 Chancellor

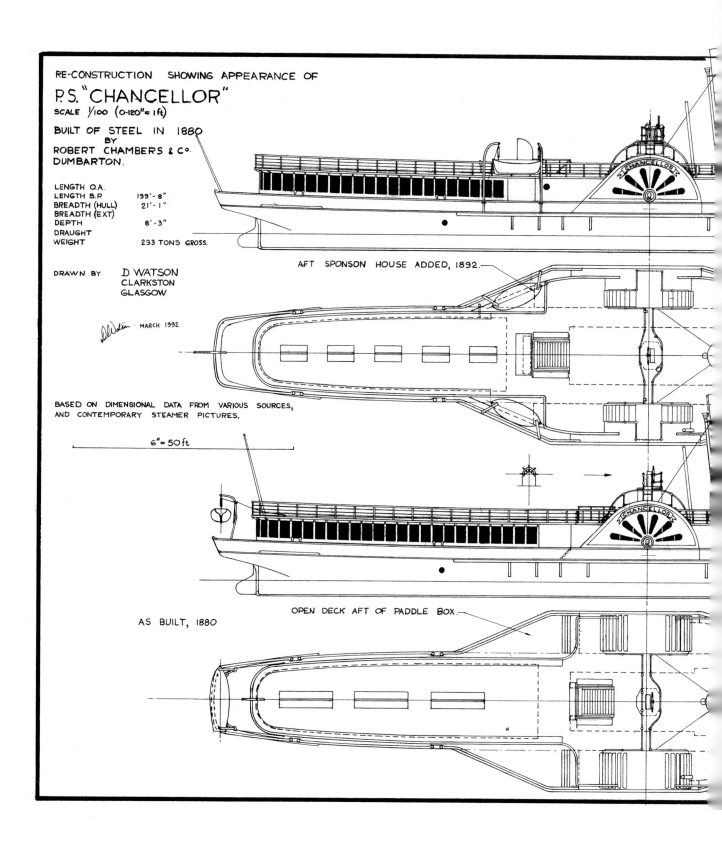

RE-CONSTRUCTION SHOWING APPEARANCE OF

P.S. "CHANCELLOR"

SCALE 1/100 (0·120"= 1 ft)

BUILT OF STEEL IN 1880
BY
ROBERT CHAMBERS & C°.
DUMBARTON.

LENGTH O.A.	
LENGTH B.P.	199'- 8"
BREADTH (HULL)	21'- 1"
BREADTH (EXT)	
DEPTH	8'- 3"
DRAUGHT	
WEIGHT	233 TONS GROSS.

DRAWN BY   D. WATSON
CLARKSTON
GLASGOW

D.Watson · MARCH 1992

BASED ON DIMENSIONAL DATA FROM VARIOUS SOURCES,
AND CONTEMPORARY STEAMER PICTURES.

6" = 50 ft

AFT SPONSON HOUSE ADDED, 1892.

OPEN DECK AFT OF PADDLE BOX.

AS BUILT, 1880

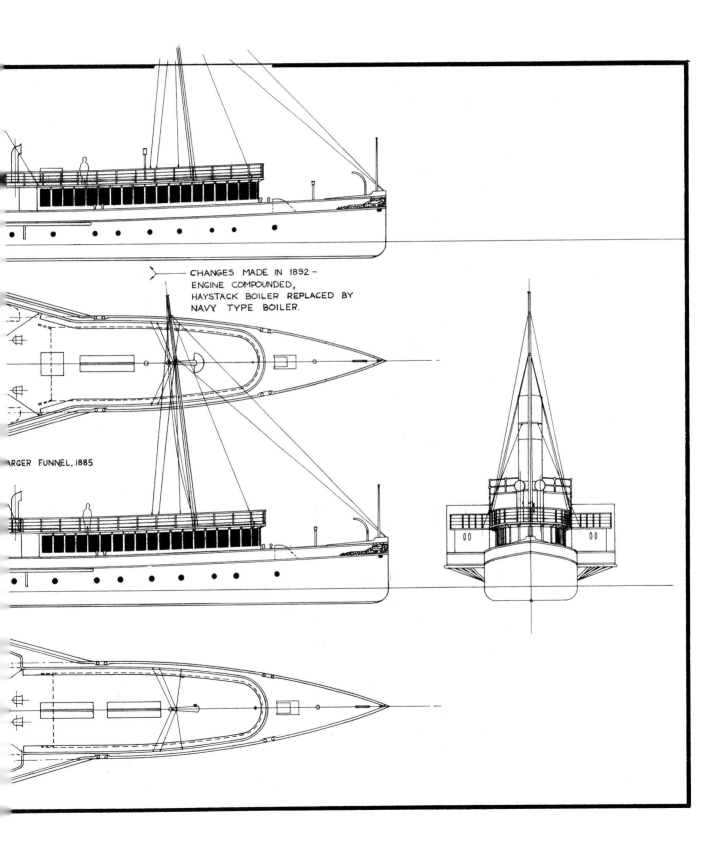

CHANGES MADE IN 1892 —
ENGINE COMPOUNDED,
HAYSTACK BOILER REPLACED BY
NAVY TYPE BOILER.

ARGER FUNNEL, 1885

Builder:	Greenock.	
Engine:	Greenock.	
Boiler:	Unknown.	
Owner:	D. Napier.	1822-1831
	City of Glasgow St. Pkt. Co.	1831-1834
Captain (1st):	Carmyle.	
Service:	Glasgow – Greenock – Douglas, I.O.M., Liverpool.	
End:	Unknown.	

THE PS *City of Glasgow* carried three masts, and had one tall slender funnel.

During her service she had a nasty incident in 1825, when on one occasion while undergoing some engine repairs at Douglas, Isle of Man, she was driven aground by strong winds, and it appeared that she might become a total loss. Fortunately this was avoided, as salvage work carried out on her enabled her to be towed back to the Clyde, where she was repaired.

The ultimate fate of the *City of Glasgow* (1822) is not known, but a second *City of Glasgow* appeared in 1835, so it must be presumed that the 1822 steamer was disposed of before that year.

Reproduced courtesy of Manx National Heritage, The Manx Museum
The City of Glasgow 1822

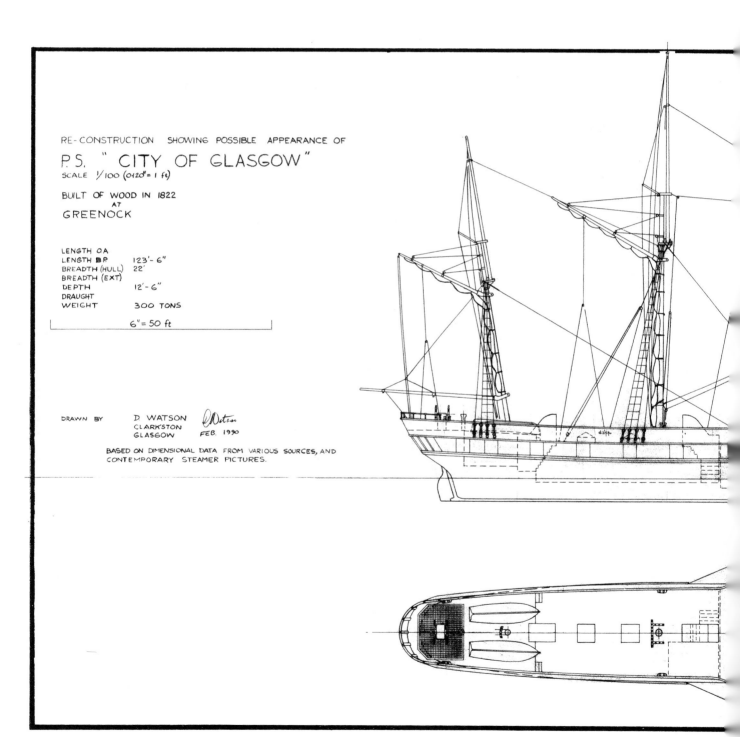

RE-CONSTRUCTION SHOWING POSSIBLE APPEARANCE OF

P.S. " CITY OF GLASGOW "
SCALE 1/100 (0·120" = 1 ft)

BUILT OF WOOD IN 1822
AT
GREENOCK

LENGTH O.A.
LENGTH B.P.   123'- 6"
BREADTH (HULL)   22'
BREADTH (EXT)
DEPTH   12'- 6"
DRAUGHT
WEIGHT   300 TONS

                6" = 50 ft

DRAWN BY   D WATSON
                 CLARKSTON
                 GLASGOW   FEB. 1990

            BASED ON DIMENSIONAL DATA FROM VARIOUS SOURCES, AND
            CONTEMPORARY STEAMER PICTURES.

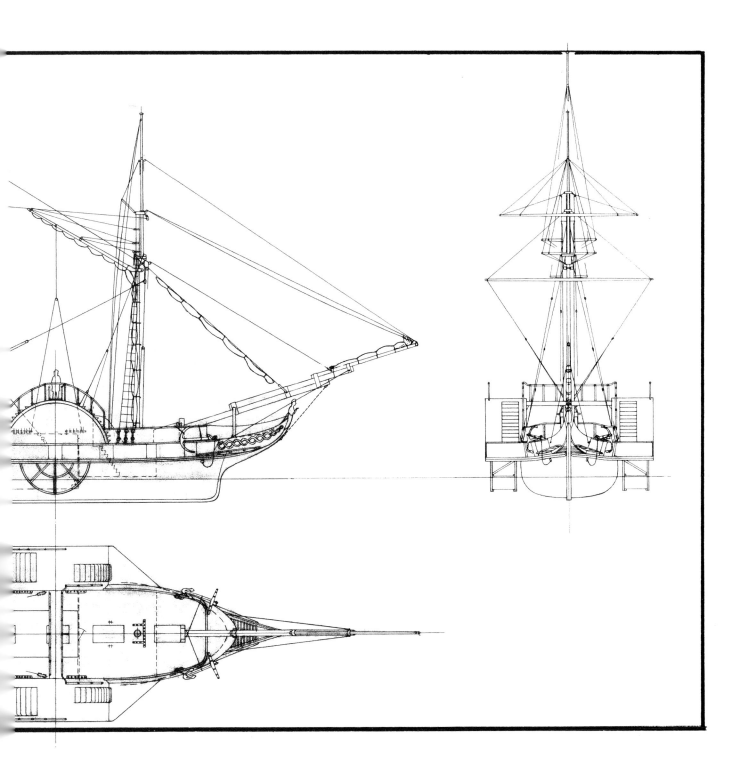

Builder:	**John Wood, Port Glasgow.**
Engine:	**John Robertson.**
Boiler:	**Unknown.**
Owner:	**John Robertson and Robert Steven**
Captain (1st):	**Captain William McKenzie.**
Service:	**Glasgow, Greenock, Gourock.**
End:	**Broken up 1828.**

THIS paddle steamer served for fifteen years on the Glasgow, Greenock, and Gourock route. During this time she had different owners and had her name changed three times, from *Clyde* to *Gourock* in 1823, to *Lord Byron* in 1825, and to *George IV* in 1826.

When built her hull cost £650 and her engine and boiler £700.

A detailed description of the PS *Clyde* appeared in the 1813 September issue of the "Glasgow Monthly Repository", which was repeated in Andrew McQueen's 1924 book "Echoes of Old Clyde Paddle Wheels".

Like many of the early river Clyde steamers, her main deck was extended out to the full width of the paddle sponsons, and this was carried along the full length of the hull, the decking being supported by timbers from the hull. She had a 25 foot high funnel which could carry a square sail, and was built with a rather flat design of hull, in order to give her a shallow draft of 33 to 36 inches.

She had a 16 feet long fore cabin, entered from the side, and a 20 feet long aft cabin, entered from the rear, with a ceiling height of 6.5 feet. The fore and aft cabins were separated by the engine room and a cargo carrying space, each about 15 feet long.

Her paddle wheels had a dip of 15 to 18 inches, were 9 feet in diameter, 4 feet wide, and carried eight iron floats.

The PS *Clyde* had a crew of five, and she could carry 250 passengers at a speed of 3 to 4.5 miles per hour.

She was withdrawn and broken up in 1828.

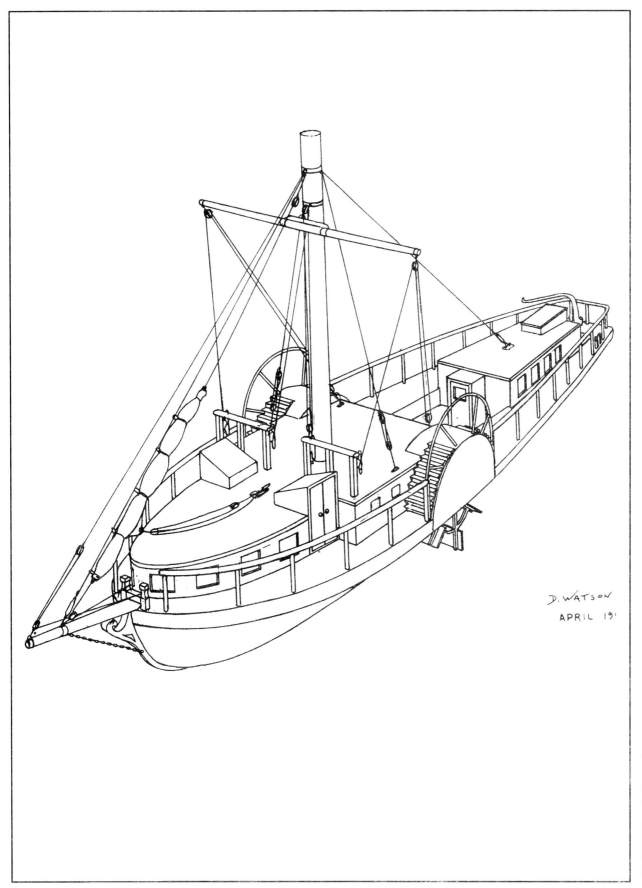

D. WATSON
APRIL 19'

RE-CONSTRUCTION SHOWING POSSIBLE APPEARANCE OF

P.S. " CLYDE "

SCALE 1/100 (0.120"= 1 ft)

BUILT OF WOOD IN 1813
BY
JOHN WOOD Cº
PORT GLASGOW

LENGTH O.A.   75'
LENGTH B.P.   68'
BREADTH (HULL)   14'
BREADTH (EXT)   24'
DEPTH   7'-6"
DRAUGHT   3'
DISPLACEMENT   65 TONS

6"= 50 Ft

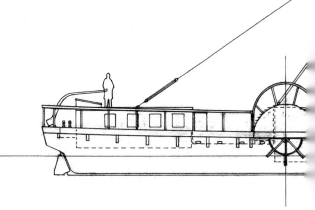

DRAWN BY   D. WATSON
                CLARKSTON
                GLASGOW   OCT. 1989

BASED ON DIMENSIONAL DATA FROM VARIOUS SOURCES, AND
CONTEMPORARY STEAMER PICTURES

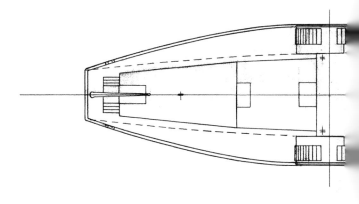

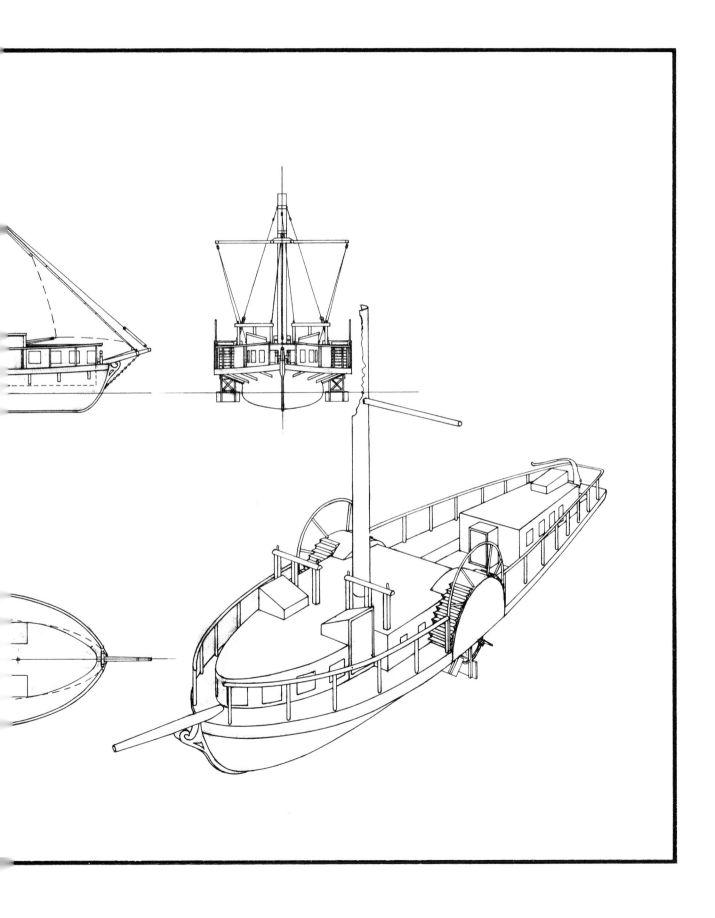

Builder:	**John Wood, Port Glasgow.**	
Engine:	**John Robertson.**	
Boiler:	**Robert Napier.**	
Owner:	**Henry Bell.**	**1812-1820**
Captain:	**James Bruce.**	
Service:	**Glasgow, Greenock, Helensburgh, then Fort William.**	
End:	**Wrecked at Craignish Point, December, 1820.**	

THE appearance of the first successful passenger carrying paddle steamer in Europe, the *Comet*, as originally built, is fairly well established. She had two four bladed paddles on individual arms on each side, her funnel carried a yard arm on which a square sail could be set, she had an open engine compartment, with the engine positioned on the starboard side, a 'sunken' cabin aft, a figurehead of a woman, and she was steered by a tiller at her square stern.

After about two months, her two four bladed paddles on each side were changed to one rimmed paddle wheel per side, and her engine cylinder (11 in. diameter, and 16 in. stroke) was changed to one of greater capacity (12.5 in. diameter and 16 in. stroke). At the same time the engine flywheel was changed from a four spoked wheel to a six spoked six feet diameter balanced wheel.

Sometime during her first year, the *Comet* was lengthened forward of the engine room, by about twenty feet. This lengthening was not registered at Custom House, where the *Comet* was first registered in May of 1813.

In 1819, she was again lengthened, this time aft of the engine room, and re-engined with a more powerful engine. On this occasion she was re-registered at Greenock Custom House, about December, 1819.

Initially, the *Comet* plied between Glasgow, Greenock and Helensburgh, as a passenger carrying steamship, but by 1816 there were other steamboats working on the river, and to avoid competition with the later, more advanced steamers, Henry Bell moved his ship to fresh waters in the Firth of Forth.

The *Comet* was brought back to the waters of the river Clyde in 1819, for lengthening and re-engining, before starting out on her new career, which was to open up the West Highlands by establishing a regular Glasgow – Fort William service, via the Crinan Canal.

It was on this service that she met her end. In December 1820, while making her way through the islands off the Craignish Peninsula, towards Crinan and the canal, she was caught in a tide race too strong for her engine and paddles to overcome. She was swept towards the rocky shore at Craignish Point, but before grounding, she broke in two just aft of the engine.

The stern portion drifted off and sank, but fortunately all the passengers and crew were rescued, as they were on the forward part, which ran on to the rocks. The engine was later salvaged from the wreck, but what subsequently happened to this engine is unclear, as there is some confusion in the various references, between this engine and the original engine installed in the ship at launch.

It is clear, however, that the engine now in the Science Museum in London is in fact, the original engine, with the increased diameter cylinder. The original, smaller bore cylinder, is now in the Scottish Maritime Museum at Irvine.

There have been many books and articles published which give information about the *Comet*, but when closely studied it is disappointing to find that there is, in fact, not really very much known in detail about this ship. It is found that many references to the *Comet* repeat the same basic information, in some cases with minor variations and ambiguities which only help to cloud the issue.

After careful examination of many references to the *Comet*, together with a few old pictures available, I have prepared drawings of her in line with the conclusions I have reached.

According to an 1848 drawing in Robert Napier's autobiography the *Comet's* engine was positioned on the starboard side of the ship. There are conflicting publications on this, but the Napier papers are the oldest reference I have found, so I have taken the starboard mounting to be the correct position.

It will be noted that, according to my conclusions, the *Comet* was lengthened twice, although there is no direct confirmation of this. The Duckworth & Langmuir book "West Highland Steamers" quotes an original, intermediate, and final length, and several other references would seem to indicate that this was the case.

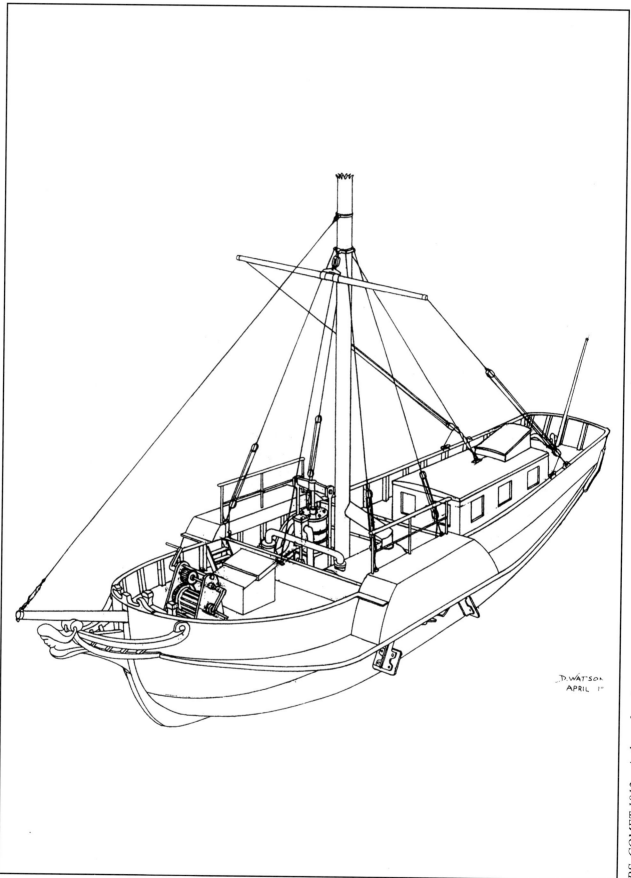

THE FIRST STEAM BOAT, THE COMET, BUILT BY
HENRY BELL, 1811
WHO BROUGHT STEAM NAVIGATION INTO PRACTICE IN EUROPE.

The Comet 1811

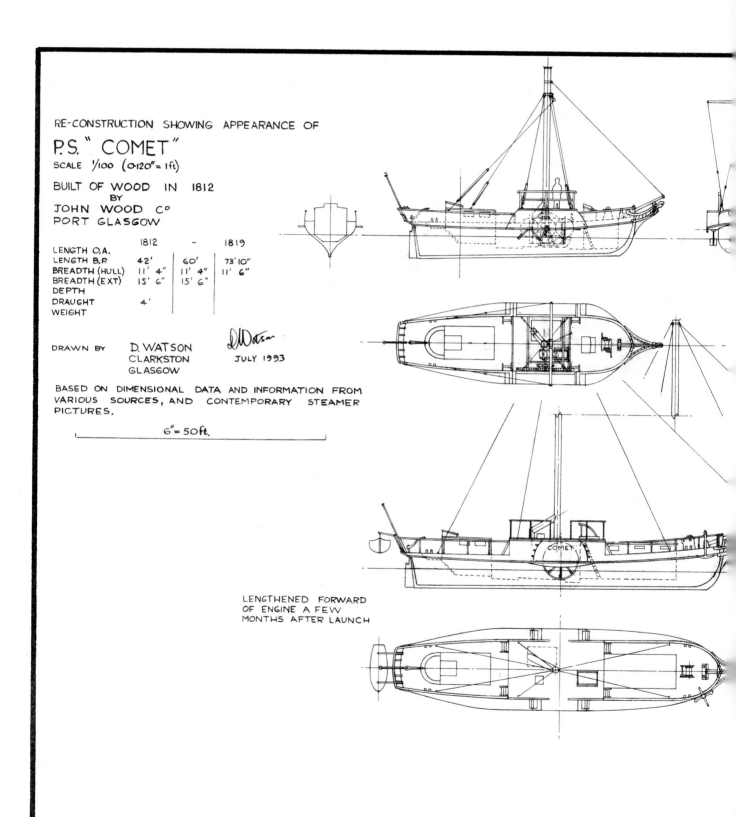

RE-CONSTRUCTION SHOWING APPEARANCE OF

P.S. " COMET "

SCALE ¹/100 (0·120"= 1ft)

BUILT OF WOOD IN 1812
BY
JOHN WOOD Cº
PORT GLASGOW

	1812	–	1819
LENGTH O.A.			
LENGTH B.P.	42'	60'	73' 10"
BREADTH (HULL)	11' 4"	11' 4"	11' 6"
BREADTH (EXT)	15' 6"	15' 6"	
DEPTH			
DRAUGHT	4'		
WEIGHT			

DRAWN BY   D. WATSON   JULY 1993
             CLARKSTON
             GLASGOW

BASED ON DIMENSIONAL DATA AND INFORMATION FROM
VARIOUS SOURCES, AND CONTEMPORARY STEAMER
PICTURES.

6"= 50ft.

LENGTHENED FORWARD
OF ENGINE A FEW
MONTHS AFTER LAUNCH

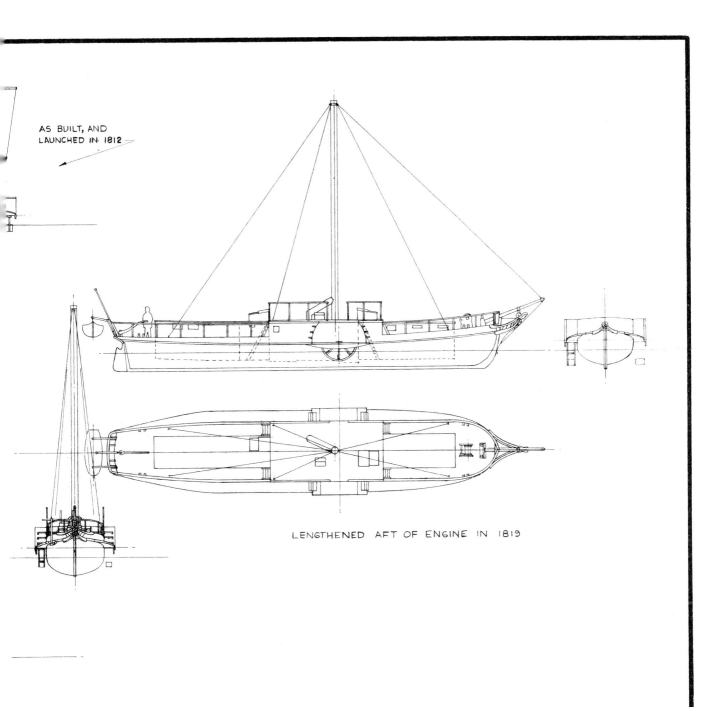

AS BUILT, AND
LAUNCHED IN 1812

LENGTHENED AFT OF ENGINE IN 1819

Builder:	**Alexander Martin & Co., Port Glasgow.**	
Engine:	**James Cook.**	
Boiler:	**Unknown.**	
Owner:	**Unknown.**	**1814**
	Messrs. R. Cheesewright & Co., London.	**1815**
Captain:	**Captain Dick.**	
Service:	**Glasgow, Greenock.**	
End:	**Broken up about 1835.**	

"A TREATISE on Propelling Vessels by Steam" by R. Buchanan, published in 1816, included drawings and layouts of the PS *Duke of Argyle*. Copies of these drawings can also be seen in the Mitchell Library's Wotherspoon Collection.

The *Duke of Argyle* plied for only about a year on the Clyde, sailing on the Glasgow – Greenock route. In 1815 she was sold to owners in London, and being too broad over the paddle boxes to pass through the Forth and Clyde Canal, she left the Clyde about May, 1815, to sail to the Thames via the West coast and the Channel.

She was the first steam vessel to sail these waters, and went first to Dublin, where she picked up some passengers, before proceeding to Wexford, further down the Irish coast. From there she went across to Milford Haven, near the tip of Wales, and then she crossed the Bristol Channel and proceeded round Lands End, up the English Channel and on to the River Thames.

When on the Thames she was renamed *Thames* and plied between London and Margate, until some time in 1816, when she was transferred to the London – Gravesend service.

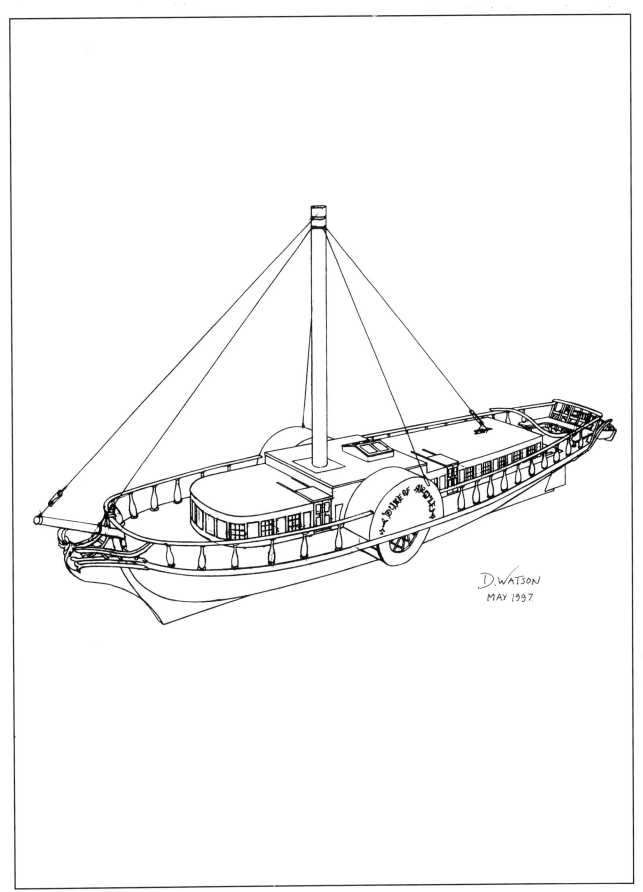

RE-CONSTRUCTION   SHOWING   APPEARANCE OF

P.S. "DUKE OF ARGYLE"

SCALE ¹/100 (0·120"= 1 ft)

BUILT OF WOOD IN 1814
BY
MARTIN   C°
PORT GLASGOW

LENGTH O.A.
LENGTH B.P.   72'
BREADTH (HULL)   14'- 6"
BREADTH (EXT)
DEPTH
DRAUGHT
WEIGHT   78 TONS

6" = 50 ft.

DRAWN BY   D. WATSON
              CLARKSTON
              GLASGOW   NOV. 1991

BASED ON DATA FROM VARIOUS SOURCES, AND
CONTEMORARY STEAMER PICTURES.

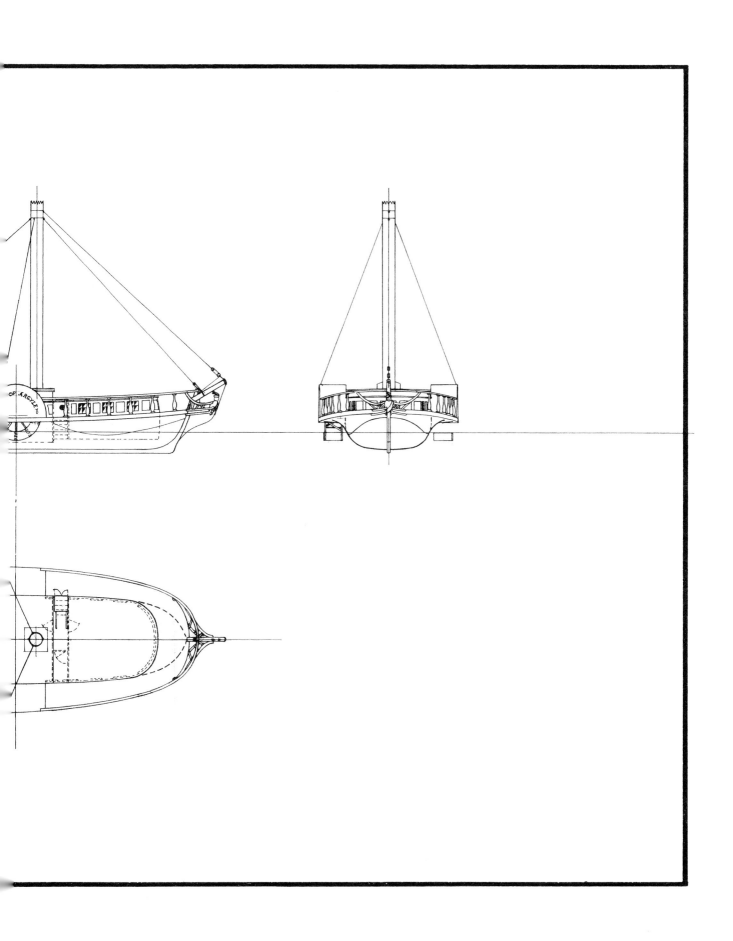

Builder:	Alex Denny.	
Engine:	McNab, Clark, Greenock.	
Boiler:	Unknown.	
Owner:	Alex Denny.	1852-1852
	Alex Williamson - Wm. Buchanan.	1852-1862
	Confederate States of America.	1862-1864
Captain:	R. Price.	
Service:	Glasgow – Rothesay – Arran – Kyles of Bute.	
End:	Sunk by Federals 1864.	

THE PS *Eagle* was a sleek two funneled steamer, the funnels being aft of the paddle boxes. She was re-boilered in 1860 and thereafter had only one funnel, still positioned aft of the paddle box. (The second *Eagle*, built in 1864, also had two funnels, but these were positioned forward of the paddle box).

For her first season she was operated by her builders, then was run by Williamson-Buchanan until 1862, when she was sold to the Confederate States of America for running the federal blockade. During her time as a confederate ship, she was re-named *Jeanette*. She was sunk by federal ships in 1864.

The *Eagle* (1852) was badly damaged in February of 1856 when hurricane force winds struck Bowling Harbour where she, and several other steamers, were laid up for the winter. She was jammed between two other steamers and was so buffetted and battered by the storm that her funnels contacted each other. She was, however, repaired and made ready in time for the summer season.

There is a model of the 1852 *Eagle* in the Glasgow Transport Museum.

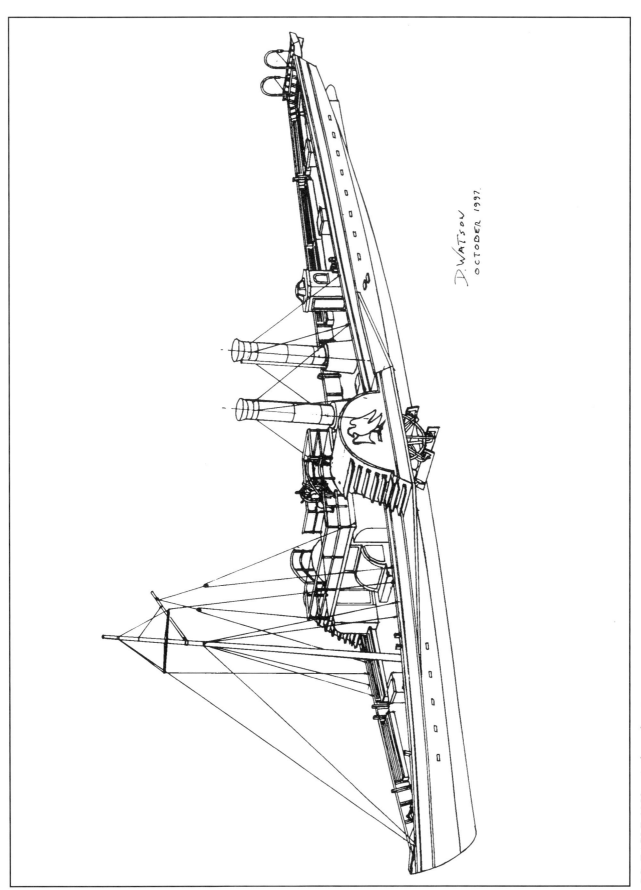

D. WATSON
OCTOBER 1997.

P.S. EAGLE 1852 – Authors drawing

P.S. "EAGLE"
SCALE 1/100 (0·120"= 1 ft)

BUILT OF IRON IN 1852
BY
ALEXANDER DENNY & BROTHER
DUMBARTON

LENGTH O.A.
LENGTH B.P.   169'- 11"
BREADTH (HULL)   16'- 6"
BREADTH (EXT)
DEPTH   8'- 4"
DRAUGHT
WEIGHT   176 TONS

6" = 50 ft

DRAWN BY   D. WATSON
              CLARKSTON
              GLASGOW   MARCH, 1990

BASED ON DIMENSIONAL DATA FROM VARIOUS SOURCES,
CONTEMPORARY STEAMER PICTURES, AND A SCALE
MODEL HELD AT THE GLASGOW MUSEUM OF TRANSPORT

RE-BOILERED IN 1860, AND FITTED
WITH ONE FUNNELL

SALOON STOVES AND GALLEY FLUES (SHOWN BELOW
IN BROKEN LINES) KNOWN FROM 1860

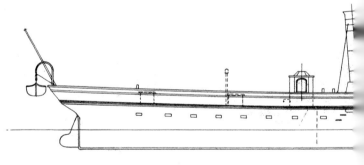

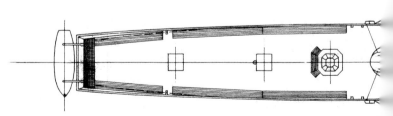

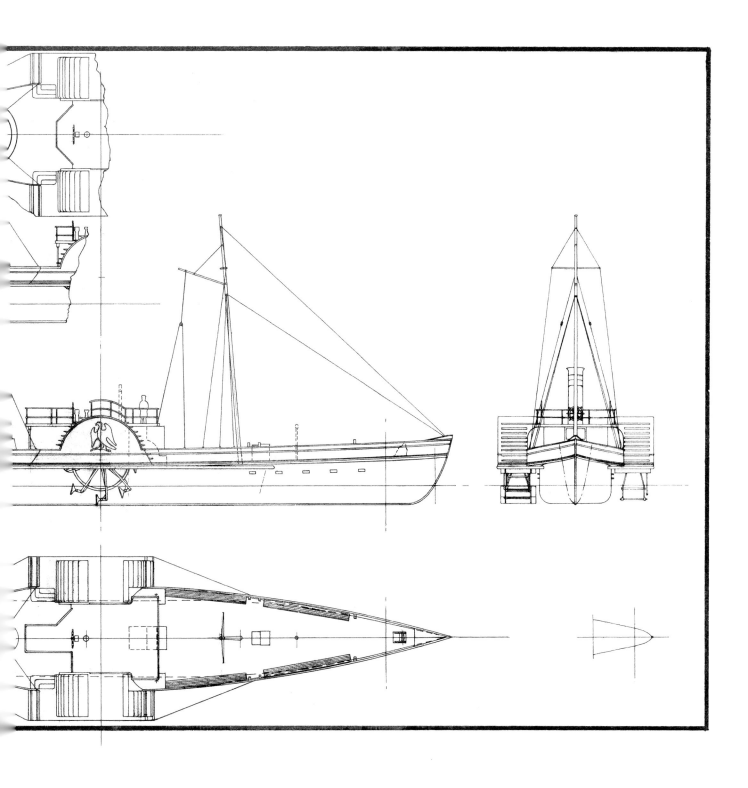

Builder:	Charles Conner & Co.	
Engine:	Anchor Line (D. & W. Henderson)	1st.
	William King & Co.	2nd.
Boiler:	Haystack.	
Owner:	William Buchanan.	1864-1894
	Ship Canal Passenger Steamer Co. (1893) Ltd.	1894-1898
	Eastham Ferry Pleasure Gardens & Hotel Co. Ltd.	1898-1899
Captain (1st):	William Buchanan.	
Service:	Glasgow – Rothesay – Arran.	
End:	Broken up 1899.	

THE 1864 PS *Eagle* was built to take the place of her predecessor, also named *Eagle*, which had been sold for blockade running. She was one of the first Clyde steamers to be designed with a raised quarter deck, i.e. the deck aft of the paddles was raised to the height of the main rail around the ship, thus giving much improved space in the aft saloon.

Originally equipped with two boilers and funnels positioned forward of the paddles, she was not generally regarded as attractive in appearance.

It would seem that the original engine, of double diagonal type, was too powerful and heavy for the hull design. Therefore, in 1866, in an effort to go some way to overcome this problem, the hull was lengthened, the additional length being aft of the paddles. Unfortunately this did not make any great improvement in the ship's performance, or coal consumption, which was said to be rather heavy. William Buchanan, however, continued to sail the *Eagle* in this condition until 1876 when the oversized engine was removed and replaced with a single diagonal engine, which was of course lighter in weight and could be suplied with steam from only one boiler.

When this change was made, she was again lengthened, this time forward of the paddles. When the *Eagle* emerged again on the Clyde, she had only one funnel, and a small cabin or saloon had been added just forward of the funnel. It was reported that the changes had resulted in reduced coal consumption, and in better performance, as well as making a great improvement in her appearance.

The alterations to the *Eagle* did not end there, for in 1887 a deck saloon was added aft of the paddles, on top of the existing raised quarter deck. She served in this condition until 1894 when she was sold to sail on the new Manchester ship canal.

Reproduced courtesy of The Mitchell Library, Glasgow City Libraries & Archives
The Eagle 1864

Reproduced courtesy of The Mitchell Library, Glasgow City Libraries & Archives
The Eagle 1864

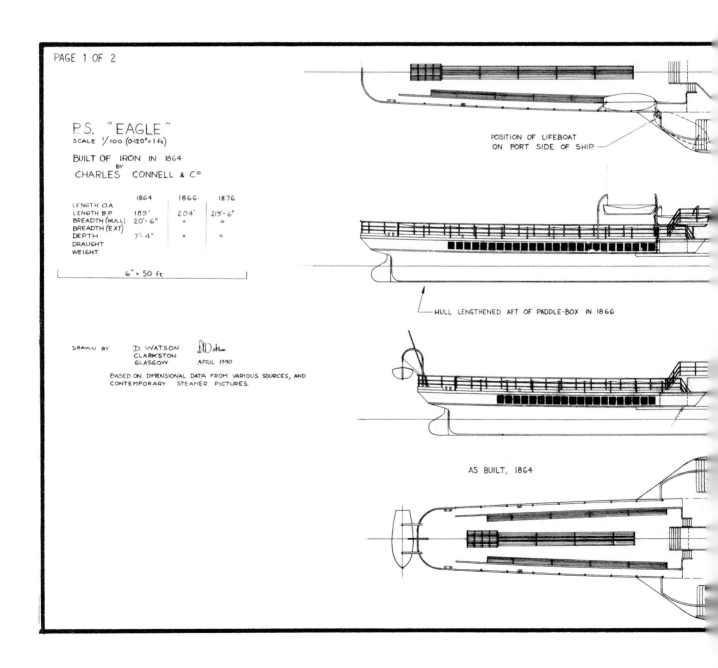

P.S. "EAGLE"
SCALE 1/100 (0·120"=1 ft)

BUILT OF IRON IN 1864
BY
CHARLES CONNELL & C°

	1864	1866	1876
LENGTH O.A			
LENGTH B.P.	189'	204'	219'-6'
BREADTH (HULL)	20'-6"	=	=
BREADTH (EXT)			
DEPTH	7'-4"	=	=
DRAUGHT			
WEIGHT			

6" = 50 ft

DRAWN BY   D. WATSON
                CLARKSTON
                GLASGOW   APRIL 1990

        BASED ON DIMENSIONAL DATA FROM VARIOUS SOURCES, AND
        CONTEMPORARY STEAMER PICTURES.

POSITION OF LIFEBOAT
ON PORT SIDE OF SHIP

HULL LENGTHENED AFT OF PADDLE-BOX IN 1866

AS BUILT, 1864

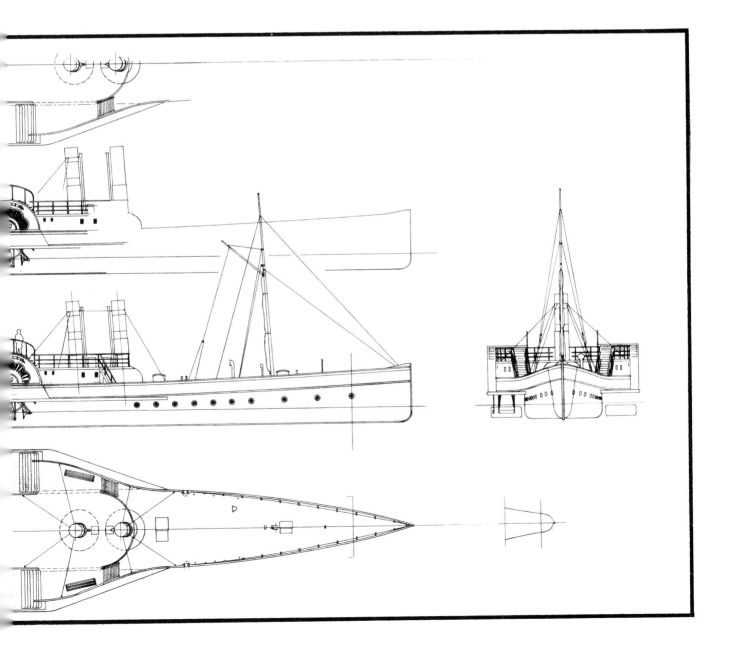

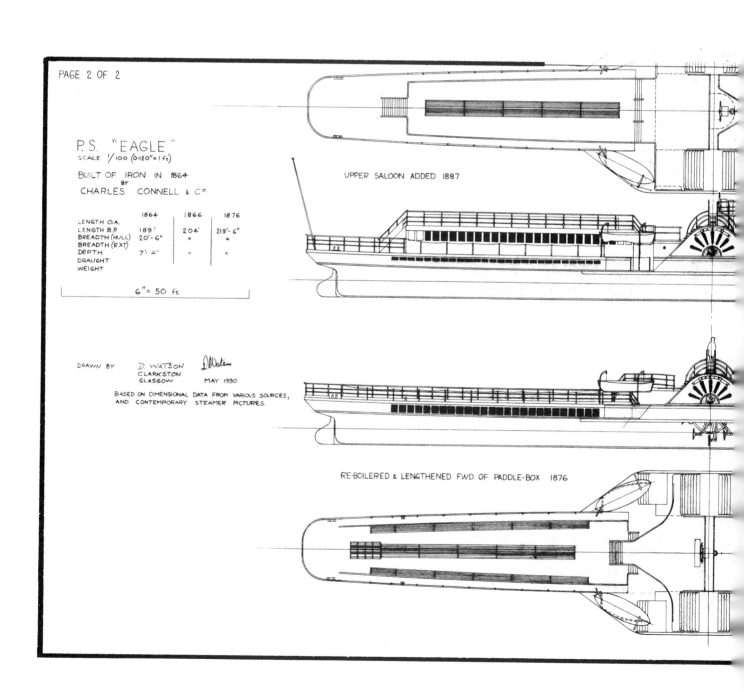

PAGE 2 OF 2

P.S. "EAGLE"
SCALE 1/100 (0·120" = 1 ft)

BUILT OF IRON IN 1864
                    BY
CHARLES   CONNELL & Cº

	1864	1866	1876
LENGTH O.A.			
LENGTH B.P.	189'	204'	219'-6"
BREADTH (HULL)	20'-6"	=	=
BREADTH (EXT)			
DEPTH	7'-4"	=	=
DRAUGHT			
WEIGHT			

6" = 50 ft

UPPER SALOON ADDED 1887

DRAWN BY   D. WATSON   DWatson
              CLARKSTON
              GLASGOW   MAY 1930

        BASED ON DIMENSIONAL DATA FROM VARIOUS SOURCES,
        AND CONTEMPORARY STEAMER PICTURES.

RE-BOILERED & LENGTHENED FWD OF PADDLE-BOX 1876

Builder:	Napier and Millar, sub-contracted from A. & J. Inglis.		
Engine:	A. & J. Inglis.		
Boiler:	A. & J. Inglis.		
Owner:	Buchanan Steamers Ltd.	April	1910-1916
	Admiralty.		1916-1919
	Buchanan Steamers Ltd.		1919-1935
	Caledonian Steam Packet Co.	October	1935-1936
	Williamson-Buchanan Stmrs. (1936) Ltd.	June	1936-1939
	Admiralty.	October	1939-1943
	Caledonian Steam Packet Co.	March	1943-1946
	B.U.		1946
Captain:	Captain Dewar.		
Service:	Dunoon, Rothesay, Kyles of Bute.		
End:	Broken up at Smith & Houston's yard, Port Glasgow, in 1946.		

THE *Eagle III*, launched on 14th April, 1910, was the third steamer named *EAGLE* to be owned by Buchanan Steamers Ltd., hence the suffix III, but was in fact the fourth steamer to carry that name. The first one, owner unknown to the author, was built in 1835, the other two, both Buchanan steamers, in 1851 and 1864.

When built, the *Eagle III* had the navigating bridge located aft of the single funnel, between the paddle boxes, which even at that time was an outdated position, and just behind that again was a long roof awning the full width of the ship, over the companionway leading down to the full width aft saloon. The roof awning was also intended to act as a raft in the event of an emergency. She had a fore mast, and short full width fore saloon, the roof of which was carried forward to the bow and formed a promenade deck which was open below. Two lifeboats were carried, one on each side just aft of the paddle sponsons, although a third lifeboat was added in 1913, after the *Titanic* disaster, mounted on the port side at the stern.

The paddle sponsons had a large number of radial vents and each carried a large ornamental eagle in the centre.

On her initial sailings she was found to be unstable when carrying a large crowd, having a severe list to one side, and from July was laid up in Bowling Harbour until the Autumn of 1910, when she was taken upriver and slipped at Pointhouse, so that the fault could be rectified. The problem was found to be in the shape of her underbody, her hull having too fine a form, which was a fault that could only be corrected by changing her hull formers.

To do this, the hull was unplated fore and aft of the engine and boiler space, and then every alternate former in these sections was removed and replaced by a new one of fuller shape. When these were securely riveted in position, the remaining formers were also changed, and thereafter the hull was replated.

After this work the *Eagle III* had no stability problems, and in fact had her passenger capacity increased by 60.

Some references indicate that the beam of the *Eagle III* was increased during this work, but this is not so, as only her hull formers fore and aft of her engine and boiler space were changed, the centre section of the hull remaining as built.

While being fitted out when requisitioned in 1916, her open fore deck was plated up, and the aft awning was removed.

In 1919, when she was reconditioned for return to civilian service, her bridge was repositioned forward of the funnel, and a small deck house was erected over the aft saloon companionway. The roof of this deck house formed an additional small observation deck, and was extended beyond the width of the deck house itself, to the full width of the ship, providing cover over the short alleyways on either side of the deck house.

The *Eagle III* was again requisitioned in 1939, renamed HMS *Oriole*, and served until 1945. She was scrapped in 1946.

Reproduced courtesy of The McLean Museum & Art Gallery, Inverclyde Council.
The Eagle III

Reproduced courtesy of The McLean Museum & Art Gallery, Inverclyde Council.
The Eagle III

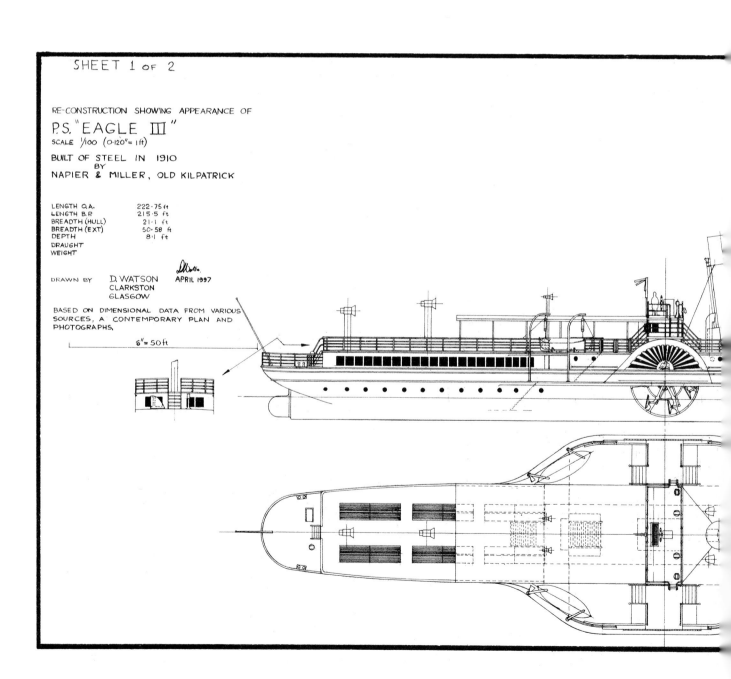

SHEET 1 OF 2

RE-CONSTRUCTION SHOWING APPEARANCE OF

P.S. "EAGLE III"
SCALE 1/100 (0·120"= 1 ft)

BUILT OF STEEL IN 1910
                  BY
NAPIER & MILLER, OLD KILPATRICK

LENGTH O.A.   222·75 ft
LENGTH B.P   215·5 ft
BREADTH (HULL)   21·1 ft
BREADTH (EXT)   50·58 ft
DEPTH   8·1 ft
DRAUGHT
WEIGHT

DRAWN BY   D. WATSON   APRIL 1997
             CLARKSTON
             GLASGOW

BASED ON DIMENSIONAL DATA FROM VARIOUS
SOURCES, A CONTEMPORARY PLAN AND
PHOTOGRAPHS.

6"= 50 ft

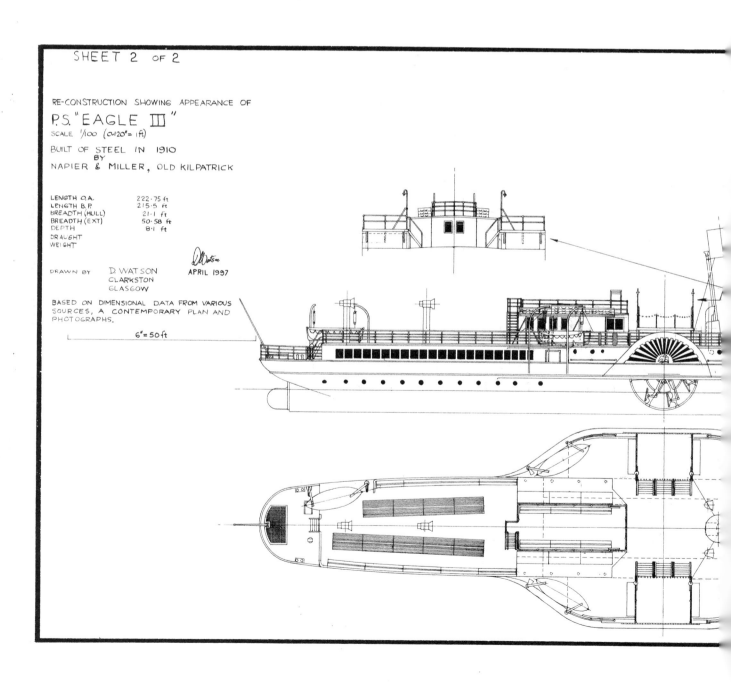

SHEET 2 OF 2

RE-CONSTRUCTION SHOWING APPEARANCE OF

P.S. "EAGLE III"

SCALE 1/100 (0·120" = 1 ft)

BUILT OF STEEL IN 1910
BY
NAPIER & MILLER, OLD KILPATRICK

LENGTH O.A.	222·75 ft
LENGTH B.P.	215·5 ft
BREADTH (HULL)	21·1 ft
BREADTH (EXT)	50·58 ft
DEPTH	8·1 ft
DRAUGHT	
WEIGHT	

DRAWN BY   D. WATSON   APRIL 1997
CLARKSTON
GLASGOW

BASED ON DIMENSIONAL DATA FROM VARIOUS
SOURCES, A CONTEMPORARY PLAN AND
PHOTOGRAPHS.

6" = 50 ft

Builder:	Smith & Rodger.	
Engine:	Smith & Rodger.	
Boiler:	Haystack – Smith & Rodger.	
Owner:	Glasgow Castle Stm. Pkt. Co.	1844-1846
	Glasgow & Liverpool Stm. Shp. Co.	1846-1851
	David Hutchison.	1851-1860
	Robert Curle, James Hamilton.	1860-1860
	David Hutchison.	1860-1879
	David MacBrayne.	1879-1905
	David MacBrayne.	1905-1927
Captain (1st):	C. Gillies.	
Service:	Glasgow – Holy Loch, then Caledonian Canal.	
End:	Broken up 1927.	

THE PS *Edinburgh Castle* as originally built, had a square stern and a slanting bow, the funnel was aft of the paddles, and she had a small poop deck. It is thought that she had the same steeple engine throughout her life of eighty three years. In 1875 she was completely overhauled and refurbished, and had major changes carried out. When she appeared again she had been renamed *Glengarry*, and her funnel and boiler were positioned forward of the paddles. She had also been lengthened forward of the paddles and had been given a straight stem, while passenger saloons had been added fore and aft.

Only the first two years of her life were spent on the Kilmun, Holy Loch run, as after that she was moved to the Caledonian Canal.

When she was finally broken up at Inverness in 1927, she was generally regarded as one of the oldest, if not **the** oldest steamer in the world.

Reproduced courtesy of The Mitchell Library, Glasgow City Libraries & Archives
The P.S. Glengarry 1844

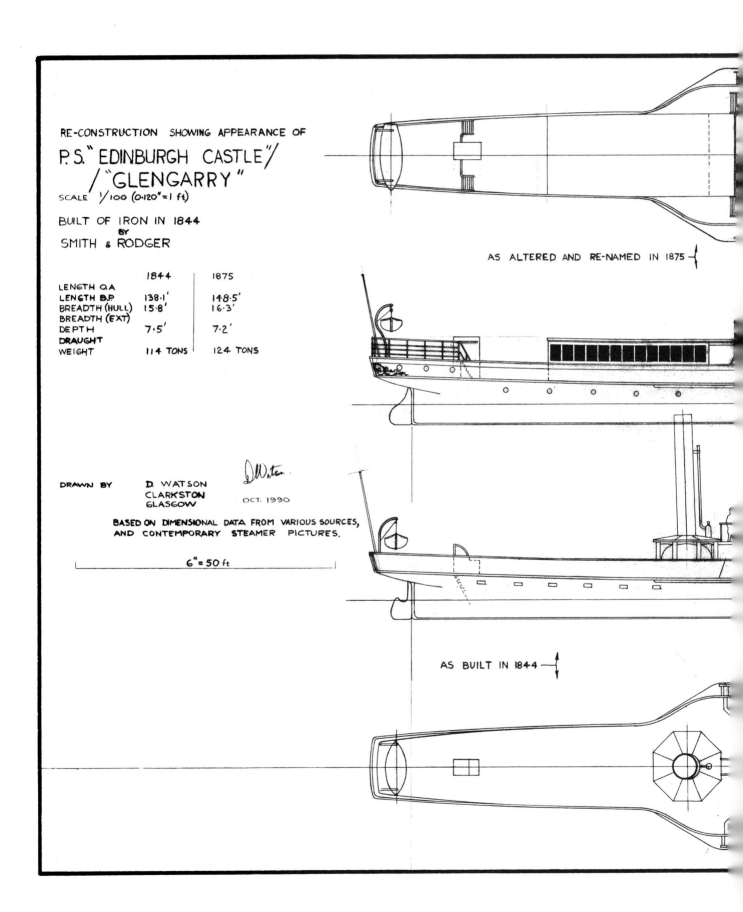

RE-CONSTRUCTION SHOWING APPEARANCE OF

P.S. "EDINBURGH CASTLE"/
/ "GLENGARRY"

SCALE ¹/₁₀₀ (0·120"= 1 ft)

BUILT OF IRON IN 1844
BY
SMITH & RODGER

	1844	1875
LENGTH O.A		
LENGTH B.P.	138·1'	148·5'
BREADTH (HULL)	15·8'	16·3'
BREADTH (EXT)		
DEPTH	7·5'	7·2'
DRAUGHT		
WEIGHT	114 TONS	124 TONS

DRAWN BY   D. WATSON
            CLARKSTON
            GLASGOW   OCT. 1990

BASED ON DIMENSIONAL DATA FROM VARIOUS SOURCES,
AND CONTEMPORARY STEAMER PICTURES.

6" = 50 ft

AS ALTERED AND RE-NAMED IN 1875

AS BUILT IN 1844

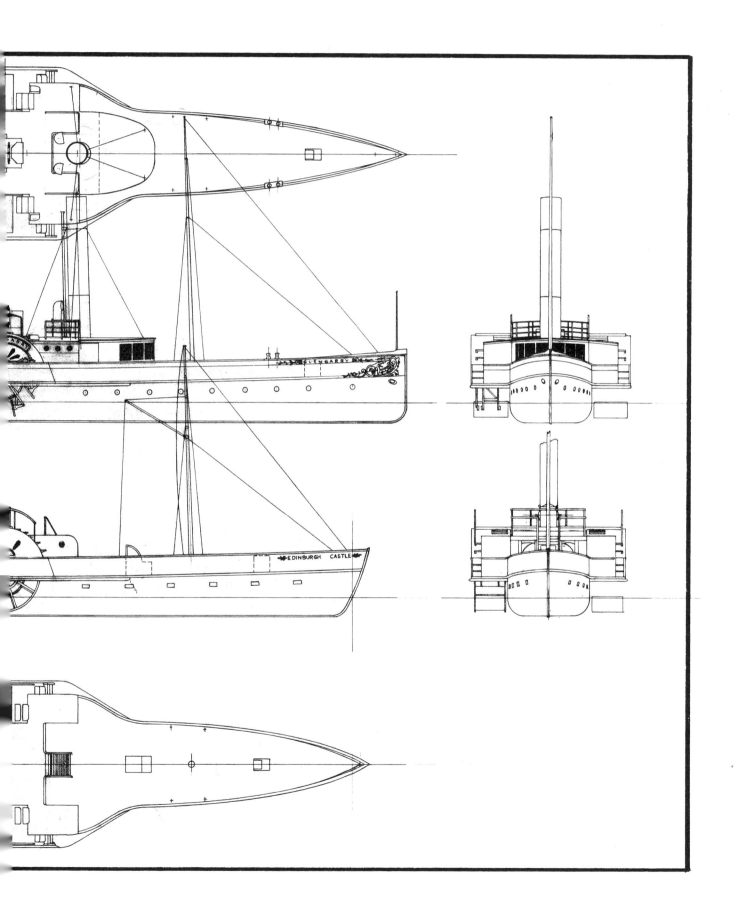

Builder:	Robert Duncan & Co., Port Glasgow.	
Engine:	Rankin & Blackmore.	
Boiler:	Haystack.	
Owner:	Loch Goil and Loch Long Stm. Boat Co.	**1879-1909**
	Loch Goil and Inverary Stm. Boat Co.	**1909-1912**
	Turbine Steamers Ltd.	**1912-1913**
Captain:	William Barr.	
Service:	Glasgow – Lochgoilhead.	
End:	Broken up 1913.	

OF all the steamers which plied on the River Clyde, the paddle wheels fitted to the 1879 *Edinburgh Castle* were the largest in diameter, and this feature it is said, was due mainly to the influence of Captain William Barr, who was to be the ship's Captain. In the opinion of many people the large paddle sponsons required made the *Edinburgh Castle* the "ugly duckling" of Clyde steamers, but the writer has never quite agreed with this point of view.

When launched in 1879, this steamer had a short promenade deck extending forward almost to the mast, which formed a partial roof over the forward main deck. This however, was left open at the sides, so any steerage class passengers were only marginally better protected against inclement weather than in the older designs of flush decked ships. This forward promenade deck was cut back soon after the initial sailings, and it is understood that this was done as it had been found to adversely affect the ship's handling qualities.

Aft of the paddles, a saloon which extended to the stern was provided, leaving a narrow alleyway along each side, as was not uncommon practice in those days.

Study of old photographs, however, show that at a later date, the promenade deck in front of the funnel was again extended forward, but only for a short distance, and with this change the space beneath was enclosed by plating up. Another change took place later with the addition of what could be a captain's cabin, or purser's office, on the promenade deck between the paddle sponsons, the roof of which was extended sideways to the sponsons, and a short distance aft, to form and awning over the companionway to the saloon below. A sheltered seat was provided at the rear of this awning.

The *Edinburgh Castle* served on the Glasgow to Lochgoilhead run for all of the thirty three years of sailing. It is thought that she was the last steamer to call at Partick Wharf before its closure in November 1906. She was withdrawn from service for scrapping in 1913.

Reproduced courtesy of The Mitchell Library, Glasgow City Libraries & Archives
The P.S. Edinburgh Castle 1879

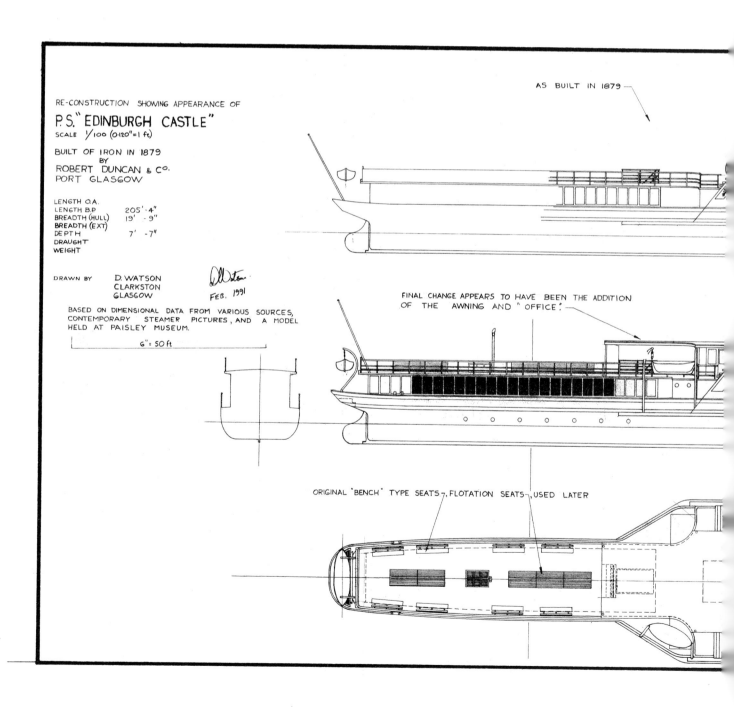

RE-CONSTRUCTION SHOWING APPEARANCE OF

P.S. "EDINBURGH CASTLE"

SCALE 1/100 (0·120"=1 ft)

BUILT OF IRON IN 1879
BY
ROBERT DUNCAN & Cº.
PORT GLASGOW

LENGTH O.A.
LENGTH B.P.   205'-4"
BREADTH (HULL)   19'-9"
BREADTH (EXT)
DEPTH   7'-7"
DRAUGHT
WEIGHT

DRAWN BY   D. WATSON
            CLARKSTON
            GLASGOW   FEB. 1991

BASED ON DIMENSIONAL DATA FROM VARIOUS SOURCES,
CONTEMPORARY STEAMER PICTURES, AND A MODEL
HELD AT PAISLEY MUSEUM.

6" = 50 ft

AS BUILT IN 1879

FINAL CHANGE APPEARS TO HAVE BEEN THE ADDITION
OF THE AWNING AND "OFFICE."

ORIGINAL "BENCH" TYPE SEATS, FLOTATION SEATS, USED LATER

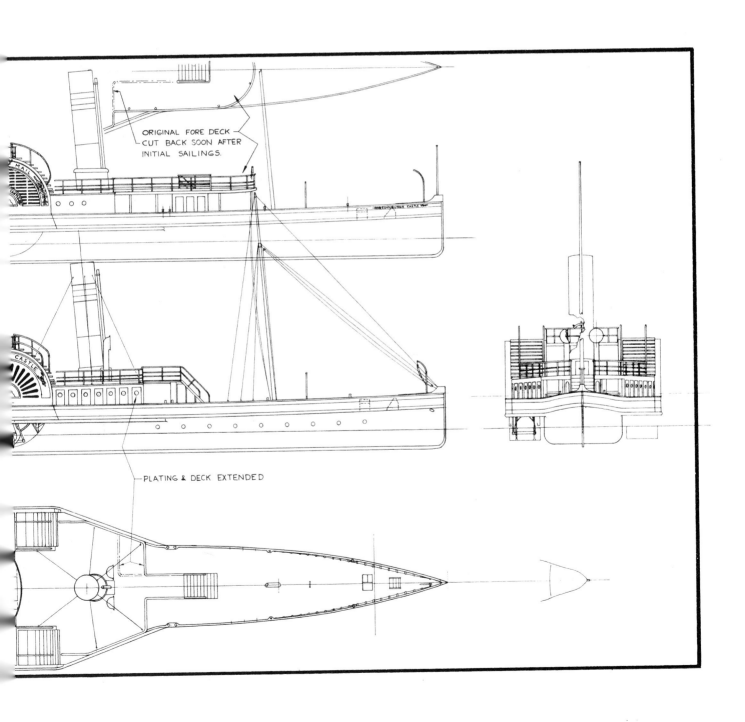

ORIGINAL FORE DECK
CUT BACK SOON AFTER
INITIAL SAILINGS.

PLATING & DECK EXTENDED

Builder:	John Wood, Port Glasgow.	
Engine:	John Thomson.	
Boiler:	Unknown.	
Owner:	Unknown.	1812-1815
	Lt. Colin Watson & Syndicate.	1815-1816
	Richard Welburn, Liverpool.	1816-1821
Captain:	Unknown.	
Service:	Glasgow, Greenock.	
End:	Unknown.	

THIS ship was the second steamboat to sail on the River Clyde, and like her predecessor, *The Comet*, she was also built by John Wood at Port Glasgow. Her engine, which was built by John Thomson, is said to be the first steam engine designed and built for a specific ship.

The *Elizabeth* had a first class saloon positioned aft of the paddles, a second class saloon forward of the paddles, while third class passengers were carried on deck, and was apparently a marked success in her Clyde service. In spite of this, or perhaps because of it, she was sold in 1815, being bought for a River Mersey syndicate by Colin Watson.

Eventually, in 1818, her engine was removed as it was thought to be unsafe, and it is understood that thereafter she had her paddles worked by horses. The final ending to her career is not known.

The PS *Elizabeth* can lay claim to several notable events, being the second practical passenger steamer in Europe, and the first to sail from the River Clyde to the River Mersey, the first to sail to the Isle of Man, and the first to ply on the waters of the River Mersey.

Andrew McQueen's book "Echoes of Old Clyde Paddle Wheels" gives a good description of the PS *Elizabeth*, and this, together with a model (made in 1932) held by the Merseyside Maritime Museum, give a good impression of the appearance of this ship.

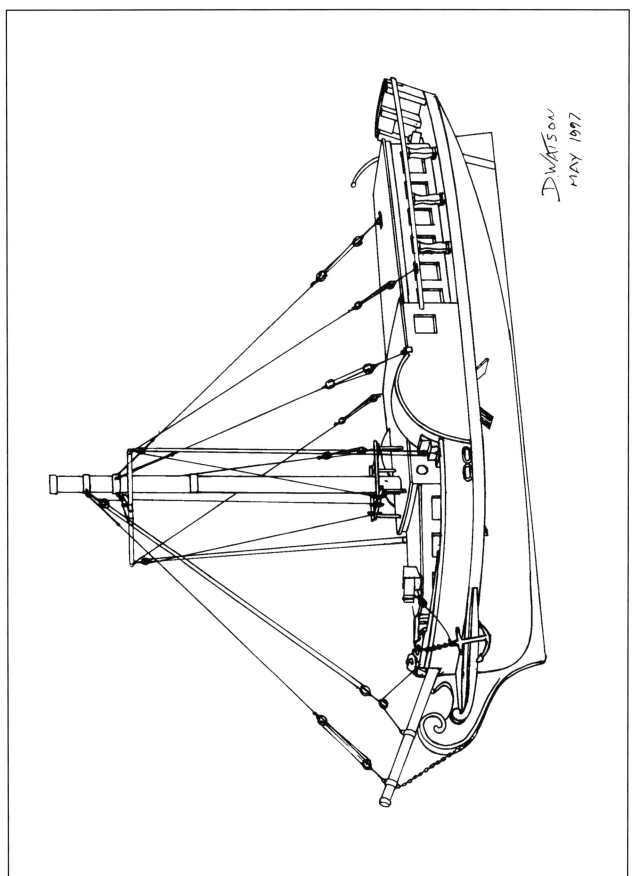

P.S. Elizabeth 1812 – Authors drawing

GENERAL ARRANGEMENT
P.S. ELIZABETH
SCALE 1/48 (1/4" = 1 ft)

BUILT OF WOOD IN 1812
BY
JOHN WOOD Cº,
PORT GLASGOW

LENGTH B.P. _____ 57 ft 9 ins
BREADTH (HULL) ____ 12 ft
BREADTH (EXT) _____ 18 ft
MLD DEPTH _____ 5 ft 9 ins
DRAUGHT _____ 4 ft
DISPLACEMENT _____ 30 Tons
                6" = 24 ft

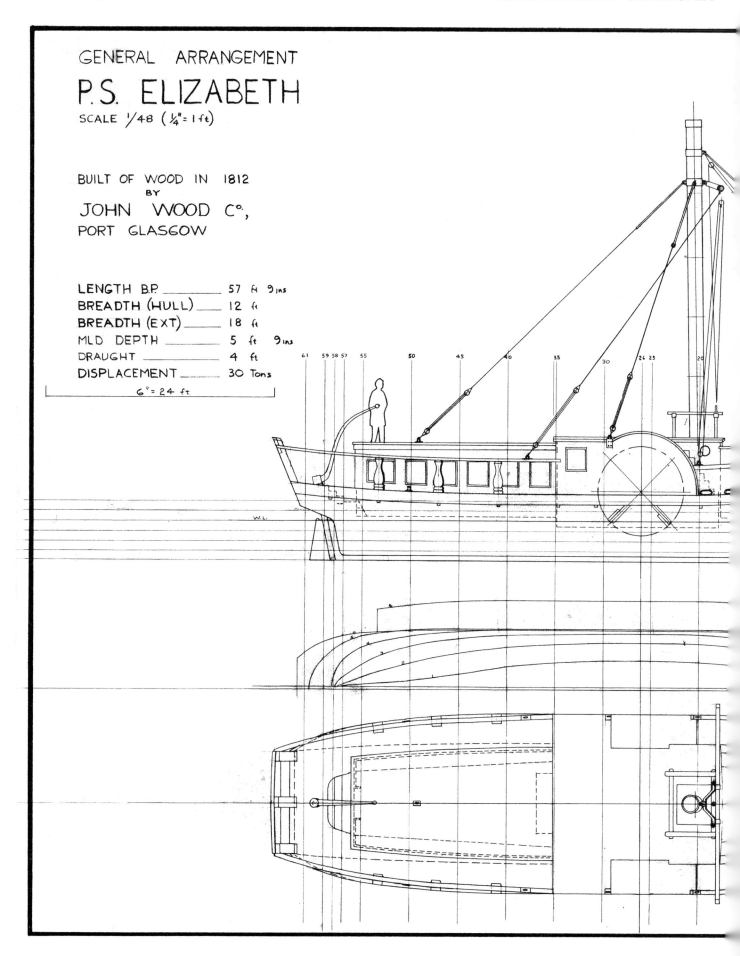

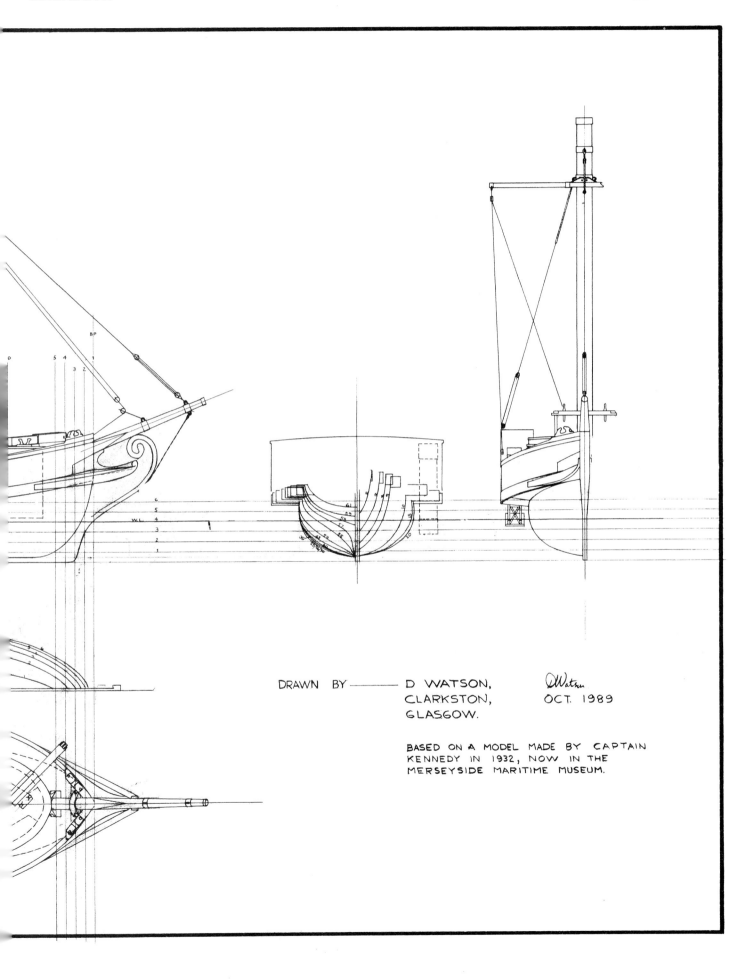

DRAWN BY ——— D WATSON,
CLARKSTON,   OCT. 1989
GLASGOW.

BASED ON A MODEL MADE BY CAPTAIN
KENNEDY IN 1932, NOW IN THE
MERSEYSIDE MARITIME MUSEUM.

Builder:	**J & G Thomson, Clydebank.**
Engine:	**Oscillating, Compound – J & G Thomson.**
Boiler:	**Navy Type, (Haystack after re-boilering).**
Owner:	**David MacBrayne.**
Captain (1st):	**John McGaw.**
Service:	**Oban, Mull, Portree, Gairloch, and Glasgow, Greenock, Ardrishaig.**
End:	**Broken up at Ardrossan in 1928.**

THE PS *Grenadier* was built at Clydebank by J & G Thomson, and delivered to David MacBrayne in 1885. The builders had turned out a beautiful ship, having two funnels, a foremast, a clipper bow with Bowsprit and carved figurehead, full width saloons with large observation windows, and a square stern. She was equipped with oscillating compound engines and two navy type boilers (also known as Scotch, or Loco boilers). Destined to serve her owners for forty two years, the *Grenadier* started off sailing from Oban to Mull, Skye, and Gairloch, and then she was switched to the Iona and Staffa run. Eventually she provided a regular service from Glasgow and Greenock to Ardrishaig in winter, and did the Iona and Staffa excursion service in summer. She could not be regarded as a fast ship, but her speed of 16 knots was fast enough for the Ardrishaig or Iona runs,

on which stations she spent most of her working life.

Although regarded as a very pretty ship from the start, her appearance was strikingly improved after her re-boilering in 1902. The fitting of two new funnels of larger diameter, set further apart, added a graceful touch to her already beautiful lines. When she was re-boilered, her navy boilers were replaced by Haystack boilers, which lasted the rest of her life. The new Haystack boilers, in fact, lasted longer than the *Grenadier* herself, one being fitted to the PS *Glencoe* in 1928, and the other to the PS *Gondolier* in 1930.

Originally equipped with one lifeboat mounted in the stern, two more were added at a later date, positioned just aft of the paddle sponson housings. After the re-boilering in 1902, the stern lifeboat was removed, leaving her with two lifeboats only, until 1913, when, after the *Titanic* disaster in 1912, two more boats were added, mounted forward of the sponson housings.

There are, however, some old photographs depicting the *Grenadier* after re-boilering, with only two lifeboats, mounted forward of the sponson housings, and carrying what appears to be some type of flotation equipment aft of the paddle sponson housing. It is likely that this condition did not last for very long, as most pictures of the *Grenadier* show her with lifeboats mounted aft of the sponson housings.

The original carved figurehead at the bow was replaced in 1907, after being damaged in a collision with another vessel.

During the 1914-18 war, the *Grenadier* was requisitioned by the Admiralty, temporarily renamed HMS *Grenade* and used for mine sweeping work. Fortunately she came through the war without mishap and returned to the Firth of Clyde in 1919 to continue her service for MacBrayne.

The end for the *Grenadier* came in 1927, in Oban, when fire broke out during the night.

The flames quickly caught hold of the soft furnishings and flammable fittings, and spread uncontrollably throughout the ship, which gradually settled to the bottom, due perhaps to buckling of the steel plates or the volume of water hosed aboard, or a combination of both. When it was over only the fire blackened funnels and saloons could be seen above water, and three of her crew had perished, one of whom was Captain Archibald McArthur. Captain McArthur had commanded the *Grenadier* for many years, and had officially retired in 1926, but had been given an advisory position when the Captain's post was taken over from him by Captain McLean.

In 1928 the *Grenadier* was raised, made seaworthy, had her paddles removed, and was towed to Greenock and then to Ardrossan, after it had been ascertained that she was beyond economical repair.

So ended the career of the PS *Grenadier*, one of the most handsome paddle steamers to sail the west coast of Scotland. The carved figurehead can still be seen in the Glasgow Museum of Transport.

Reproduced courtesy of The Scottish Maritime Museum.
The Grenadier 1885

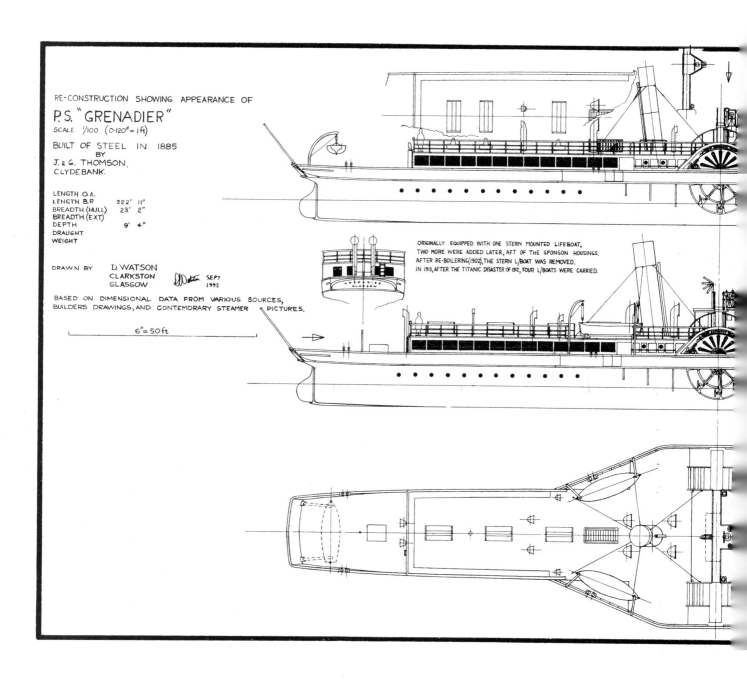

RE-CONSTRUCTION SHOWING APPEARANCE OF

P.S. "GRENADIER"

SCALE 1/100 (0·120"= 1 ft)

BUILT OF STEEL IN 1885
BY
J. & G. THOMSON,
CLYDEBANK.

LENGTH O.A.
LENGTH B.P   222' 11"
BREADTH (HULL)   23' 2"
BREADTH (EXT)
DEPTH   9' 4"
DRAUGHT
WEIGHT

DRAWN BY   D. WATSON
            CLARKSTON
            GLASGOW   SEPT
                             1992

BASED ON DIMENSIONAL DATA FROM VARIOUS SOURCES,
BUILDERS DRAWINGS, AND CONTEMORARY STEAMER PICTURES.

6"= 50 ft

ORIGINALLY EQUIPPED WITH ONE STERN MOUNTED LIFEBOAT,
TWO MORE WERE ADDED LATER, AFT OF THE SPONSON HOUSINGS.
AFTER RE-BOILERING (1902), THE STERN L/BOAT WAS REMOVED.
IN 1913, AFTER THE TITANIC DISASTER OF 1912, FOUR L/BOATS WERE CARRIED.

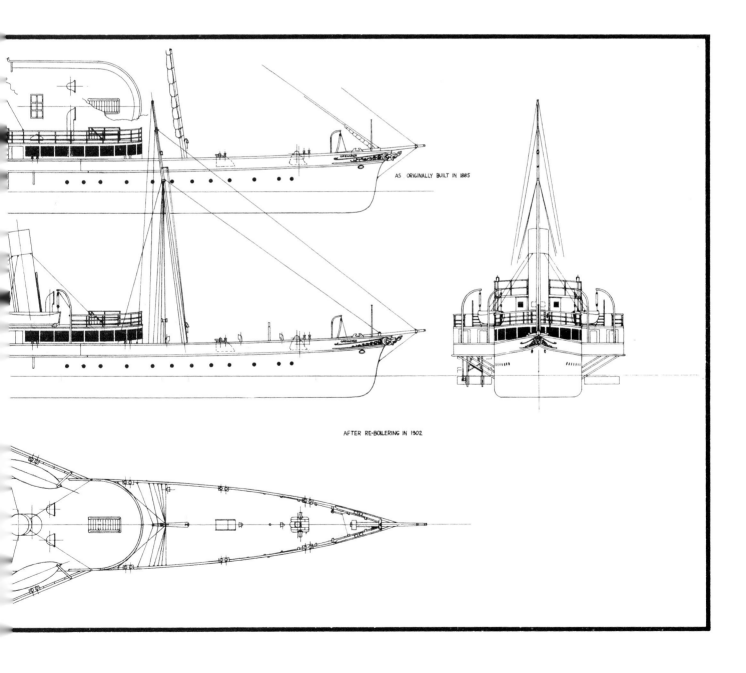

AS ORIGINALLY BUILT IN 1885

AFTER RE-BOILERING IN 1902

Builder:	**William Fyfe, Fairlie.**	
Engine:	**George Dobie, Tradeston.**	**1st.**
	Caird & Co., Greenock.	**2nd.**
Boiler:	**Unknown.**	
Owner:	**John Henderson, Wm. Croil, Dugald McPhee.**	**1814-18--**
	Clyde Shipping Co.	
Captain:	**Unknown.**	
Service:	**Glasgow, Greenock.**	
End:	**1873.**	

THE PS *Industry* spent most of her working life, of 59 years, as a cargo boat, with occasional use as a lighter, or a tug, although it is likely that some passengers were carried from time to time. During her life she always plied under her given name, never having had a name change, as happened with so many of her contemporaries. Being a cargo boat, she did not have any passenger saloons, but had the paddle wheel sponsons extended from stem to stern, giving ample deck space.

The original side lever engine, by George Dobie, was replaced in 1828 by a new engine built by Caird & Co.

About 1857 she was completely overhauled, and at that time was fitted with a folding funnel, enabling her to sail up river of Glasgow Bridge. Some time after her overhaul, she struck an underwater obstacle, near Renfrew,

and sank, but was raised and repaired, and carried on working her trade for a further sixteen years.

The *Industry* was finally laid up about 1873 in Bowling Harbour, and never sailed again. Her timbers eventually rotted and when it was at last recognised that she was the oldest steamer in the world, it was too late for any attempt at salvage and preservation. Her engine, however, was saved, and after many years in Kelvingrove Park, and in storage, it is now the property of the Scottish Maritime Museum, Irvine. It will be displayed there when the new exhibition hall (ex, Stephen Co's, Engine Shop) is completed.

There are a number of photographs and pictures in the Glasgow Mitchell Library's Wotherspoon Collection and elsewhere, which illustrate this ship.

Reproduced courtesy of The Mitchell Library, Glasgow City Libraries & Archives
The Industry 1813

RE-CONSTRUCTION   SHOWING   POSSIBLE   APPEARANCE OF

P.S. " INDUSTRY "

SCALE ¹/₁₀₀ (0·120"= 1 ft)

BUILT OF WOOD IN 1813
BY
WILLIAM FIFE C°
FAIRLIE

LENGTH O.A.
LENGTH B.P.   67'
BREADTH (HULL)   14'-8"
BREADTH (EXT)
DEPTH   8'-1"
DRAUGHT
WEIGHT   53 TONS

6" = 50 ft

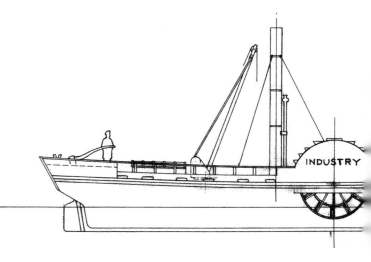

DRAWN BY   D. WATSON   *DWatson*
                CLARKSTON   · DEC. 1989
                GLASGOW

        BASED ON DIMENSIONAL DATA FROM VARIOUS
        SOURCES, PHOTOGRAPHS, AND CONTEMPORARY
        STEAMER PICTURES.

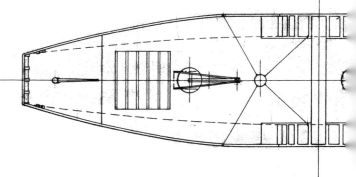

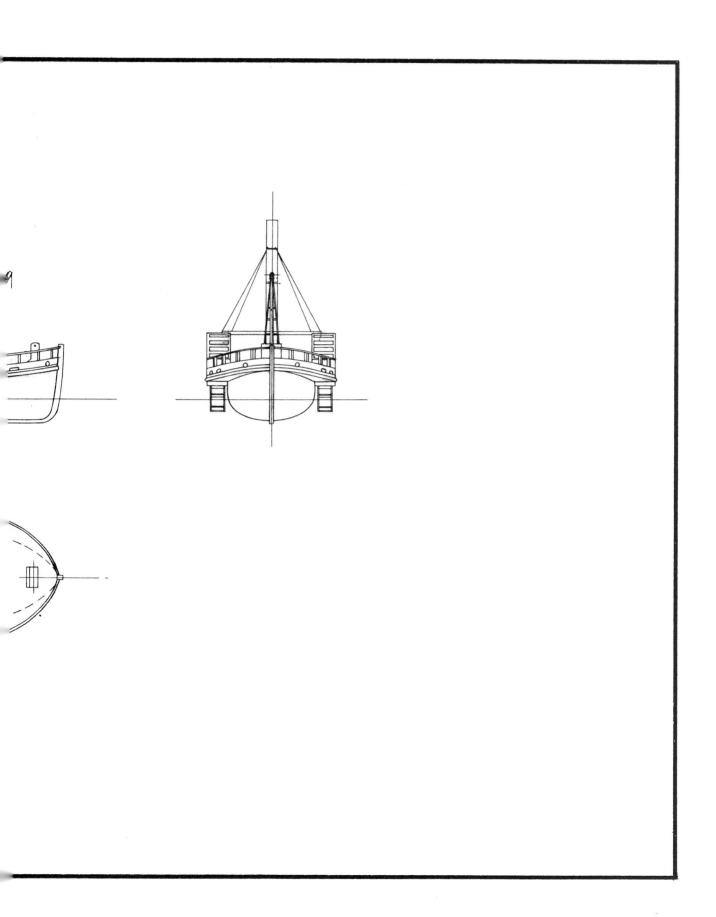

Builder:	John Wood, Port Glasgow.	
Engine:	David Napier, side lever engine.	
Boiler:	2 Copper-Flue.	
Owner:	Inverary Castle Stm. Pkt. Co.	1820-1832
	Castle Stm. Pkt. Co.	1832-18-?
	Alexander Barlas.	? -1836
Captain (1st):	Captain Dug Thompson.	
Service:	Glasgow, Rothesay, Loch Fyne.	
End:	Broken up 1836.	

THIS was a smart clipper bowed steamship, with one funnel positioned aft of the paddles, and two masts. She was, in fact, the second ship of the name, the first having been built in 1814.

Her route was Glasgow, Rothesay, and Loch Fyne, although it is recorded that in 1828 she sailed to Brodick on some days.

While in the service of Alexander Barlas, in 1836, Oban was her base, from where she sailed to Tobermory, Staffa, and Iona.

There is a picture of her in the Glasgow Mitchell Library Wotherspoon Collection.

Reproduced courtesy of The Mitchell Library, Glasgow City Libraries & Archives
The Inverary Castle 1820

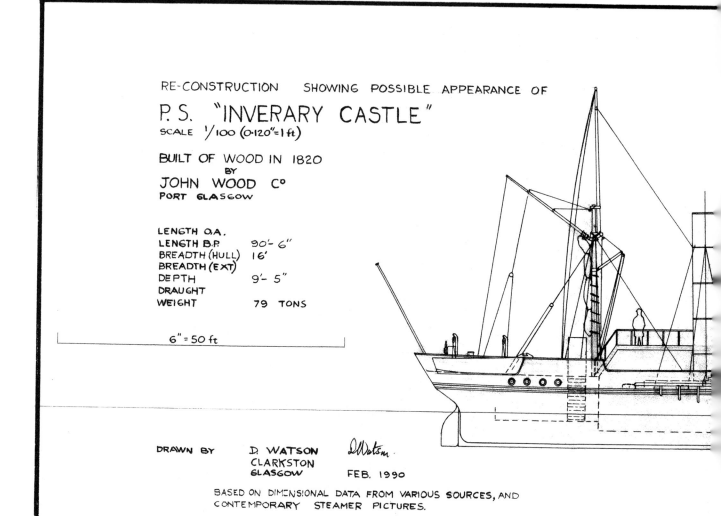

RE-CONSTRUCTION   SHOWING POSSIBLE APPEARANCE OF

P.S. "INVERARY CASTLE"
SCALE ¹/₁₀₀ (0·120"=1 ft)

BUILT OF WOOD IN 1820
BY
JOHN WOOD Cº
PORT GLASGOW

LENGTH O.A.
LENGTH B.P.   90'- 6"
BREADTH (HULL) 16'
BREADTH (EXT)
DEPTH   9'- 5"
DRAUGHT
WEIGHT   79 TONS

6" = 50 ft

DRAWN BY   D. WATSON
              CLARKSTON
              GLASGOW   FEB. 1990

BASED ON DIMENSIONAL DATA FROM VARIOUS SOURCES, AND
CONTEMPORARY STEAMER PICTURES.

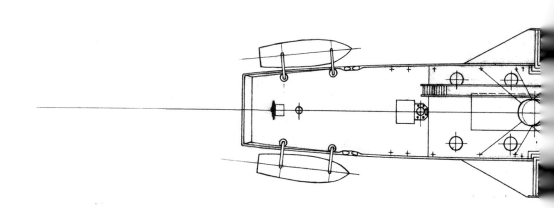

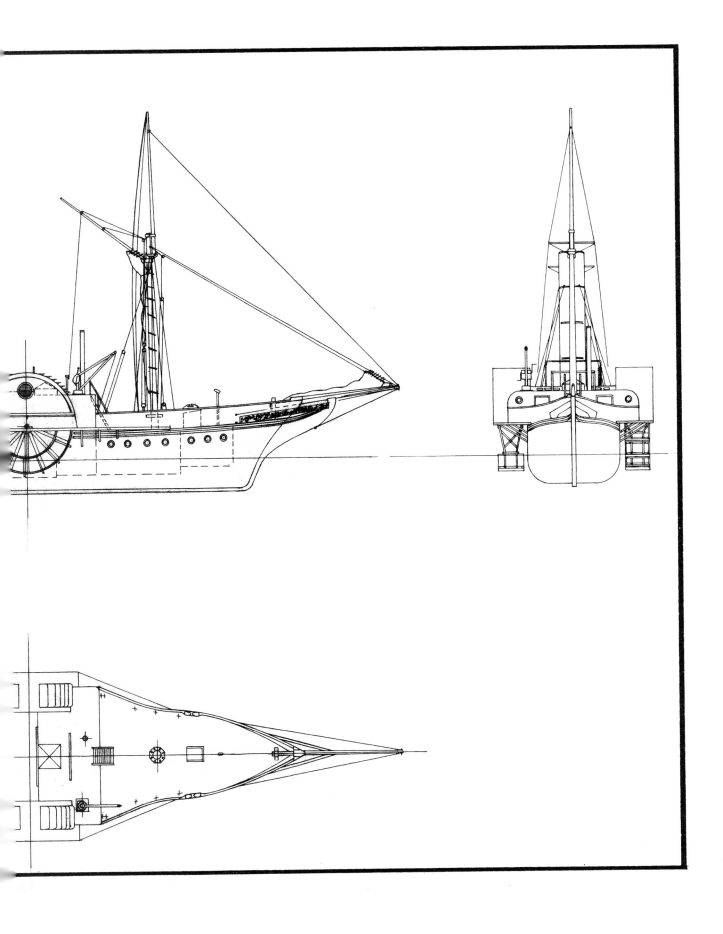

Builder:	Tod & McGregor, Mavisbank.	
Engine:	Steeple (ex PS *Tarbert Castle*, 1838).	
Boiler:	Haystack.	
Owner:	Castle Steam Pkt. Co.	1839-1842
	Glasgow Castle Steam Pkt. Co.	1842-1846
	Glasgow & Liverpool Stmship. Co.	1846-1851
	William Denny & Bros.	1851-1851
	Glasgow & Lochfyne Stm. Pkt. Co.	1851-1857
	David Hutcheson & Co.	1857-1879
	David MacBrayne & Co.	1879-1895
Captain (1st):	Donald Currie.	
Service:	Glasgow, Greenock, Loch Fyne and Inverary.	
End:	Broken up at Bowling, 1892-1895.	

THE first and second ships named *Inverary Castle* were built in 1814 and 1820 respectively. This vessel, the third *Inverary Castle*, was, to the writer's knowledge, the last paddle steamer to carry this name.

The PS *Inverary Castle* was built by Tod & McGregor, Mavisbank, Glasgow, and it is said that she was the first steamer built by them at their yard at Mavisbank. She was fitted with a haystack boiler and had a steeple engine salvaged from the steamer *Tarbert Castle* of 1838, which had been wrecked on the 17th January, 1839, on the Silver Rocks, Ardmarnock Beach, Kilfinan Bay, across Loch Fyne from Lochgilphead. This engine lasted all her life.

When first registered, the *Inverary Castle* had two masts, was schooner rigged, had a standing bowsprit, a woman figurehead, a single funnel positioned just aft of her paddles, a poop deck with a mock gallery, and had fixed floats on her paddles.

Mock galleries were not uncommon at that time, and would have been included to enhance the appearance of what was an ordinary Scottish west coast general cargo ship. Her fixed floats were replaced with feathering floats in May 1868.

At her bows, the deck was raised to the level of the main rail, forming a low fo'castle, and a guard rail up to the bows was provided around this area.

She was lengthened twice during her life, firstly in 1862, at which time her poop deck and mock gallery were removed, and then again in 1873, when she was also reboiled. A deck saloon was added at the stern after lengthening.

In her original condition she would have had two lifeboats, one mounted at each side of her poop deck. When the poop deck was removed at her first lengthening, these were replaced by a single, stern mounted lifeboat.

In her final condition she had raised walkways from the bridge between the paddle boxes, extending fore and aft over the cargo holds, and offset to port. A 'flying bridge' was added between and above the paddle boxes at some time after her final lengthening.

The *Inverary Castle* was initially built for the Castle Steam Pkt. Co., and her primary duties were the carrying of cargo between Glasgow and the Loch Fyne Ports, although passengers would also be carried occasionally. After several changes of ownership, she ended her career, which lasted 53 years, in the red funnel fleet of David MacBrayne, still serving on the same route on which she had started.

While in the service of David Hucheson & Co., on one occasion in November 1864, when she was on her way down the River Clyde, she was passing the Clyde Street Ferry just as the ferry, a passenger carrying row boat, was leaving the ferry steps. The ferry was loaded down almost to the gunwales, and the wash from the *Inverary Castle's* non-feathering paddles caused the overloaded ferry to capsize. At least nineteen lives were lost, but the exact number was never accurately determined. Less than a year after the accident a steam powered ferry boat replaced the rowing boat.

Another incident involving the *Inveraray Castle* occurred on January 13th, 1877 (note that the change in the spelling of the name was officially recorded on 25th August, 1874). On that occasion the steamer *Lady Gertrude* was approaching Toward Pier when a mechanical failure of the engine reverse signal mechanism caused the steamer to continue past the pier. She was caught by the wind and blown in towards the pier, which her stern struck, causing her bows to swing shorewards, where she went aground. Happily, the passengers were able to be landed from the stern of the *Lady Gertrude*. The *Inveraray Castle* was passing at the time, and made an attempt to tow the *Lady Gertrude* off the rocks, but was unsuccessful in this. Further attempts by tugs also failed to save the *Lady Gertrude*, and she eventually sank and broke in two. Her engine was salvaged and used in a new steamer.

The *Inveraray Castle* virtually spent her whole career serving the same route on which she started, with only a few exceptions, such as the season in 1859 when she carried cargo round the Mull of Kintyre to Oban. This was done because the normal canal boat service from Ardrishaig to Crinan was suspended, due to closure of the Crinan Canal after the disaster in February of that year, when the swollen reservoirs in the hills of Knapdale, which feed the canal, had burst their banks and swept down into the canal, carrying tons of earth and rubble.

She was eventually laid up, and in 1892, was being broken up at Bowling. This must have been a slow process, it seems, as it is reported that her hull was still there in 1895.

Reproduced from an original held by Mr A. Fraser, Bishopton

The Inverary Castle 1839

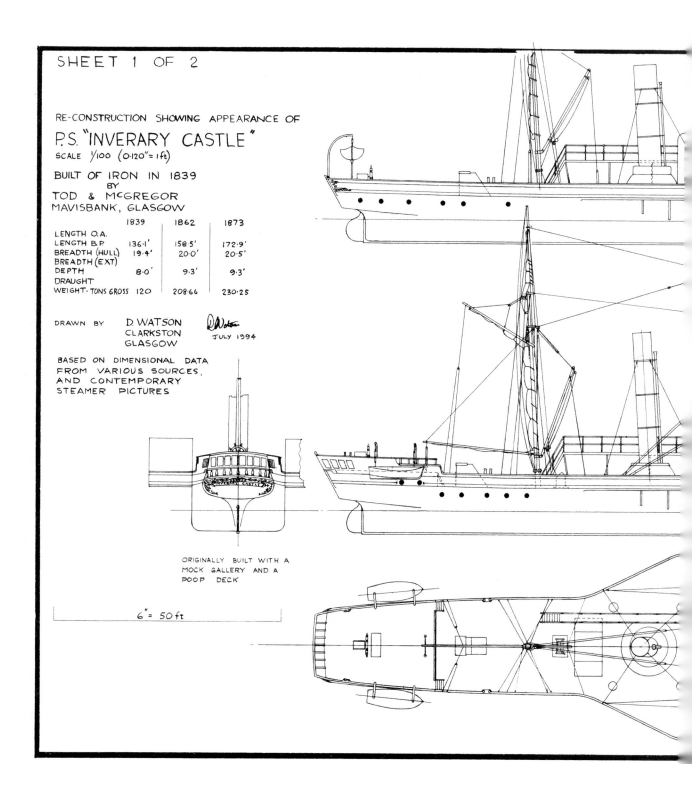

SHEET 1 OF 2

RE-CONSTRUCTION SHOWING APPEARANCE OF
P.S. "INVERARY CASTLE"
SCALE 1/100 (0.120"= 1 ft)

BUILT OF IRON IN 1839
BY
TOD & McGREGOR
MAVISBANK, GLASGOW

	1839	1862	1873
LENGTH O.A.			
LENGTH B.P.	136.1'	158.5'	172.9'
BREADTH (HULL)	19.4'	20.0'	20.5'
BREADTH (EXT)			
DEPTH	8.0'	9.3'	9.3'
DRAUGHT			
WEIGHT-TONS GROSS	120	208.66	230.25

DRAWN BY   D. WATSON
CLARKSTON
GLASGOW   JULY 1994

BASED ON DIMENSIONAL DATA
FROM VARIOUS SOURCES,
AND CONTEMPORARY
STEAMER PICTURES

ORIGINALLY BUILT WITH A
MOCK GALLERY AND A
POOP DECK

6" = 50 ft

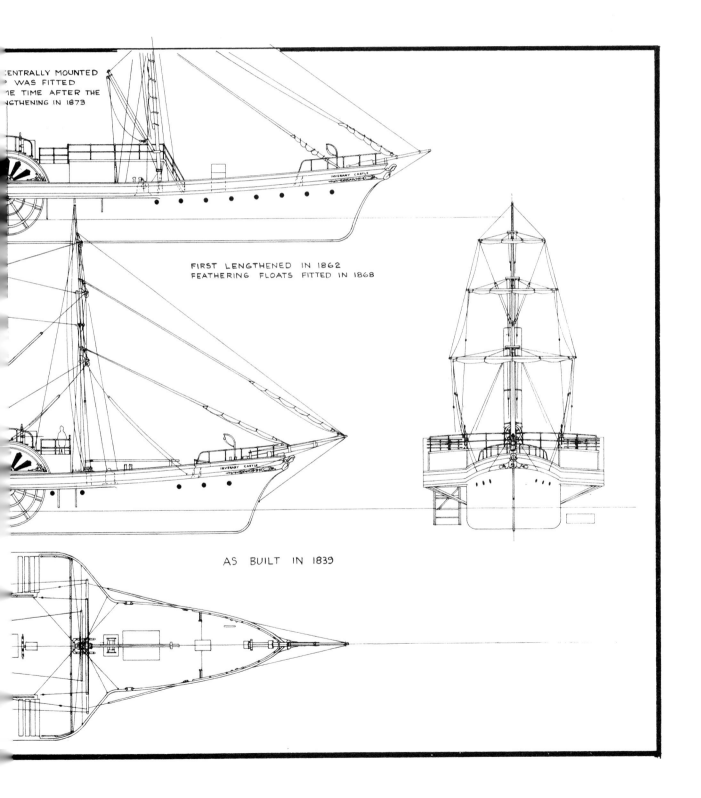

CENTRALLY MOUNTED
P WAS FITTED
ME TIME AFTER THE
NGTHENING IN 1873

FIRST LENGTHENED IN 1862
FEATHERING FLOATS FITTED IN 1868

AS BUILT IN 1839

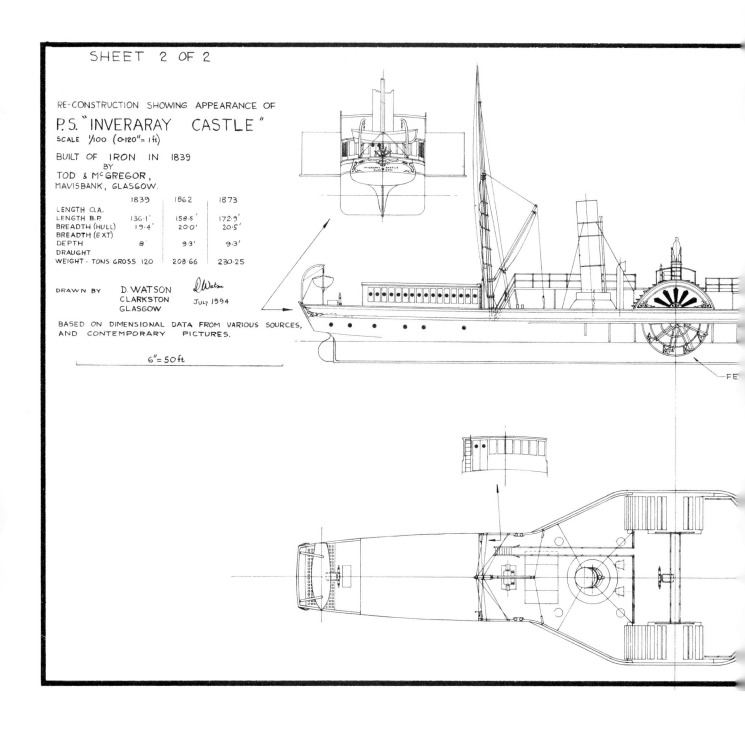

SHEET 2 OF 2

RE-CONSTRUCTION SHOWING APPEARANCE OF
P.S. "INVERARAY CASTLE"
SCALE 1/100 (0·120"= 1 ft)

BUILT OF IRON IN 1839
            BY
TOD & McGREGOR,
MAVISBANK, GLASGOW.

	1839	1862	1873
LENGTH O.A.			
LENGTH B.P.	136·1'	158·5'	172·9'
BREADTH (HULL)	19·4'	20·0'	20·5'
BREADTH (EXT)			
DEPTH	8'	9·3'	9·3'
DRAUGHT			
WEIGHT - TONS GROSS	120	208·66	230·25

DRAWN BY   D. WATSON
                CLARKSTON   JULY 1994
                GLASGOW

BASED ON DIMENSIONAL DATA FROM VARIOUS SOURCES,
AND CONTEMPORARY PICTURES.

6"= 50 ft

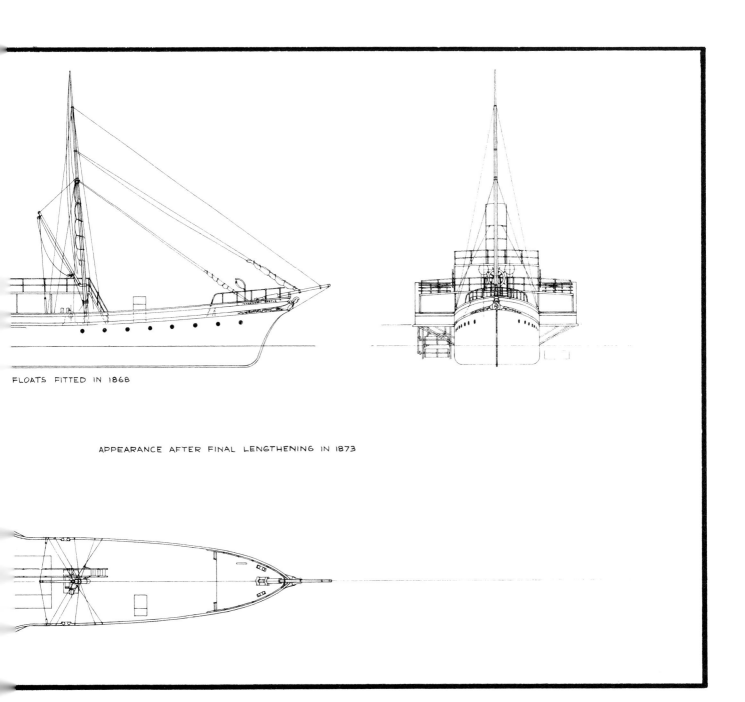

FLOATS FITTED IN 1868

APPEARANCE AFTER FINAL LENGTHENING IN 1873

Builder:	**J & G Thomson, Govan.**
Engine:	**Oscillating, J & G Thomson.**
Boiler:	**Horizontal.**
Owner:	**David Hutchison & Co.**
Captain (1st):	**Captain McGowan.**
Service:	**Ardrishaig, Glasgow.**
End:	**Sunk in collision, Gourock Bay 1862.**

DAVID Hutchison & Co., who operated steamers on the west coast of Scotland, had successfully developed the passenger and cargo trade between Glasgow and Ardrishaig with their ships, the paddle steamers *Pioneer* (1844), and *Mountaineer* (1852) to such an extent that in the 1850's it became obvious that an improved service was necessary. It was decided that a new ship was required, and the order for this was placed with J & G Thomson, who had built the PS *Mountaineer*. The new paddle steamer, named *Iona*, was launched from their Govan yard in April 1855.

Although it could not be known at the time, the Iona was to be the first of three crack steamers, all named *Iona*, and all from the same builders, and each one better than the one before.

The *Iona* of 1855 produced by the builders was a beautiful flush decked steamer with a rakish curved bow, a single mast, two funnels, and a square stern. She was powered by a simple oscillating engine, had horizontal boilers, and could steam at 17 knots.

For eight summers the *Iona* served on the Glasgow – Ardrishaig station, that is until the summer of 1862, after which, in October of that year, she was sold.

In April 1861 President Lincoln in the Americas, conducting the war against the Confederate Southern States, had ordered the naval blockade of the southern seaports. If the Southern States were to be able to continue the war, it was essential that they be able to carry on trading, and to do this, fast, shallow draught ships able to 'run the blockade' of the Northern States vessels, were needed. The Clyde river steamer was ideally suited for this task, being both fast and shallow draught, with the additional advantage of having a low profile.

It was for this blockade running work that the PS *Iona* of 1855 was sold. She was however, destined never to leave the waters of the Clyde. After being stripped of unnecessary fittings, painted grey, fitted with a main mast, and loaded with coal and provisions for the ocean crossing, she had completed compass adjustment in the Gareloch and was making her way across the Firth of Clyde on the evening of 2nd October 1862 prior to setting out on her journey across to Nassau in the Bahamas, when at about 7pm she was rammed on the starboard side, about 12ft aft of the paddle box. Such was the force of the impact that the bows of the other vessel cut through the hull of the *Iona* to within 2ft of the port side.

With such damage the *Iona* could not remain afloat, so began to sink, going down by the stern, and after about 20 minutes she disappeared beneath the surface. She sank in about 15 fathoms, but not before all persons on board had managed to transfer to the ship which had rammed her. This was the new screw steamer *Chanticleer*, which had spent the day doing trials, and was making her way back to port when she struck the *Iona*.

The cause of the ramming is not clear, but in essence it would appear that, while both ships were carrying lights, the *Iona* seems to have unexpectedly cut across the bows of the *Chanticleer* making the collision unavoidable. It has also been reported that most of the crew of the Iona were intoxicated to some extent when picked up by the *Chanticleer*.

The wreck of the *Iona* was advertised for sale in the following year, and she was eventually sold for salvage to a Glasgow man for £95. He never raised her however, probably the depth of water, about 90 feet, proved too great for the salvage capabilities of that time.

The wreck still lies in the waters off Greenock, and in recent years has been visited by divers, who tell us that only the middle section remains, where the paddle wheels, engine, boilers, and bases of the two funnels can still be seen. It appears that the stern section broke away at the time of sinking, and may lie somewhere nearby.

So ended the career of the first PS *Iona*, a steamer which, together with the two ships of the same name which followed her, set a new standard for ships of this class.

If ever you walk or drive along Greenock esplanade, and you look out across the water towards Rosneath or Kilcreggan, you can let your mind wander beneath the surface of the water, to where the PS *Iona* lies on the sea bed and think of her summer days 130 years ago when she daily plied between Ardrishaig and Glasgow.

The P.S. Iona 1855 – Authors drawing

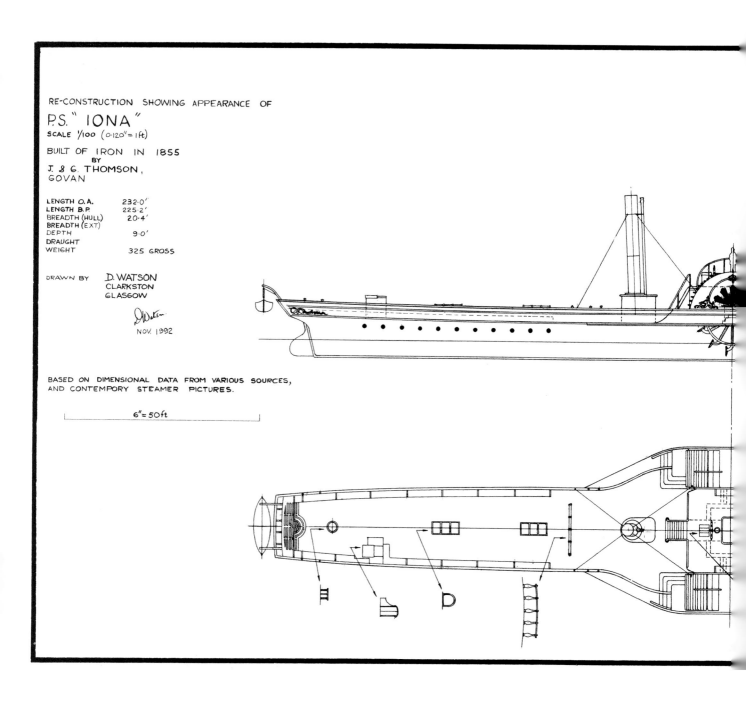

RE-CONSTRUCTION SHOWING APPEARANCE OF

P.S. " IONA "

SCALE ¹/₁₀₀ (0·120" = 1 ft)

BUILT OF IRON IN 1855
BY
J. & G. THOMSON,
GOVAN

LENGTH O.A.	232·0'
LENGTH B.P.	225·2'
BREADTH (HULL)	20·4'
BREADTH (EXT)	
DEPTH	9·0'
DRAUGHT	
WEIGHT	325 GROSS

DRAWN BY   D. WATSON
CLARKSTON
GLASGOW

NOV. 1992

BASED ON DIMENSIONAL DATA FROM VARIOUS SOURCES,
AND CONTEMPORY STEAMER PICTURES.

6" = 50 ft

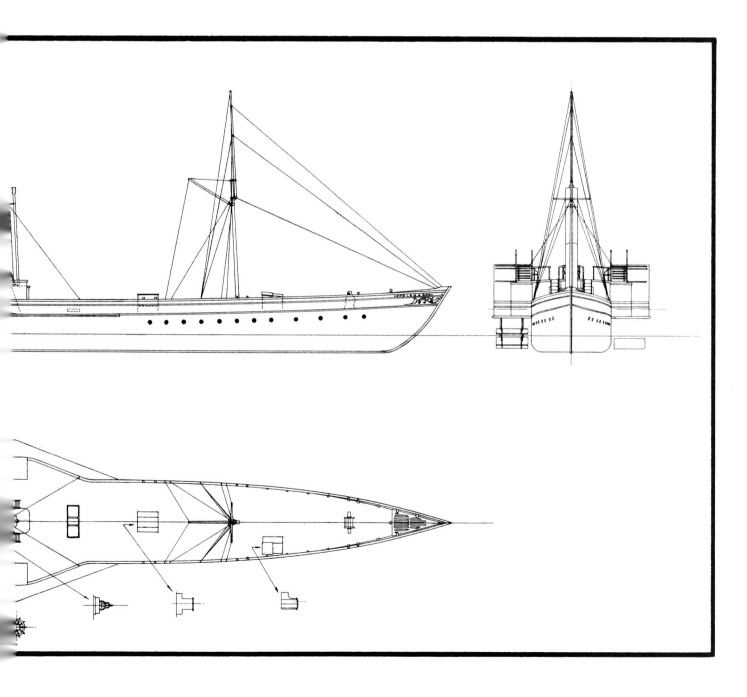

Builder:	J & G Thomson, Govan.	
Engine:	Oscillating, J & G Thomson.	
Boiler:	Horizontal.	
Owner:	David Huchison & Co.	1863-1863
	D. McNutt.	1863-1863
	Charles Hopkins Boster, Confederate	
	Southern States of America.	1863-1864
Captain:	McGowan.	
Service:	Glasgow, Ardrishaig.	
End:	Sold to the Confederate States, 1863, lost off Lundy Island, Bristol Channel, February, 1864.	

THE *Iona* of 1863 was the second ship of the name, and was built to replace the first *Iona*, (1855).

She operated on the same Clyde – Ardrishaig route, and in appearance she was very much like her predecessor, except that, unlike the older ship, she was fitted with deck saloons fore and aft. She had a curved, slanting bow, two rather squat, dumpy funnels set quite far apart, and a square stern. Like many ships of the time, she was decorated with gilded lines and scrollwork on her bows, paddlebox, and stern.

Her deck saloons, which were fitted with curtained, opening windows, were narrower than the hull, leaving alleyways around the vessel. Somewhere amidships, between the saloons, a post office was positioned, and the roof of the saloons formed a promenade deck.

She was fitted with feathering floats, and companionways (stairs) were mounted fore and aft from the main deck alleyways to the top of the paddle boxes. This last item, concerning the paddle box companionways, is a conclusion reached by the writer after examination of many pictures illustrating both the *Iona* of 1863 (*Iona II*) of and of 1864 (*Iona III*). There are no paddlebox companionways on any picture of the *Iona (III)* that the writer has seen, but on paintings and drawings of the *Iona II* these can be seen.

The helmsman aboard the *Iona (II)*, standing at the ships wheel, was positioned between the paddle boxes, on the main deck, there being no bridge on the ship as built. She was one of the earliest ships to have an engine room that was open to the view of the passengers, a feature which was to be seen in many paddle steamers built in later years.

The *Iona (II)* lasted for only one season, however, and was sold at the end of the summer of 1863 to the same buyers as her predecessor, namely, the Confederate States of America, for blockade running during the American Civil War.

For the trip to the American States the *Iona* was stripped of her deck saloons, had her hull strengthened for the crossing, was given a mainmast, loaded with provisions and coal, and set out on January 19th 1864.

She sailed from the Firth of Clyde and went down the Irish Sea heading for Queenstown, on the South East Irish coast, at which port she stopped to top up her coal stores prior to the Atlantic run. While there some trouble arose with the crew, who were charged with mutiny.

Eventually all was ready, and the *Iona* set off on her journey westwards. The weather was bad, and worsened as she sailed on, until finally, after continuous pounding by heavy seas, she began to take on water, so that her pumps were kept hard at work. The captain decided to return and run for shelter at Milford Haven, on the Welsh Coast. She proceeded towards the Bristol Channel, until, just off Lundy Island, the boiler fires were swamped and the ship began to founder. Fortunately for the crew, one of the Bristol pilot boats was able to take them all off the helpless ship, and within the hour she had sunk.

Thus ended the short career of the second PS *Iona*, a ship whose sailing operations would probably have lasted well into the twentieth century were it not for the far reaching effect of the American Civil War.

The *Iona (II)* was replaced in 1864, by the third *Iona*, from the same builders, and operated on the same route as both her predecessors. The new *Iona* was almost identical in appearance to the *Iona (II)*, and sailed on the Clyde from 1864 to 1936, when she was eventually broken up.

Reproduced courtesy of The Burrel Collection, Glasgow Museums.
The P.S. Iona II 1863

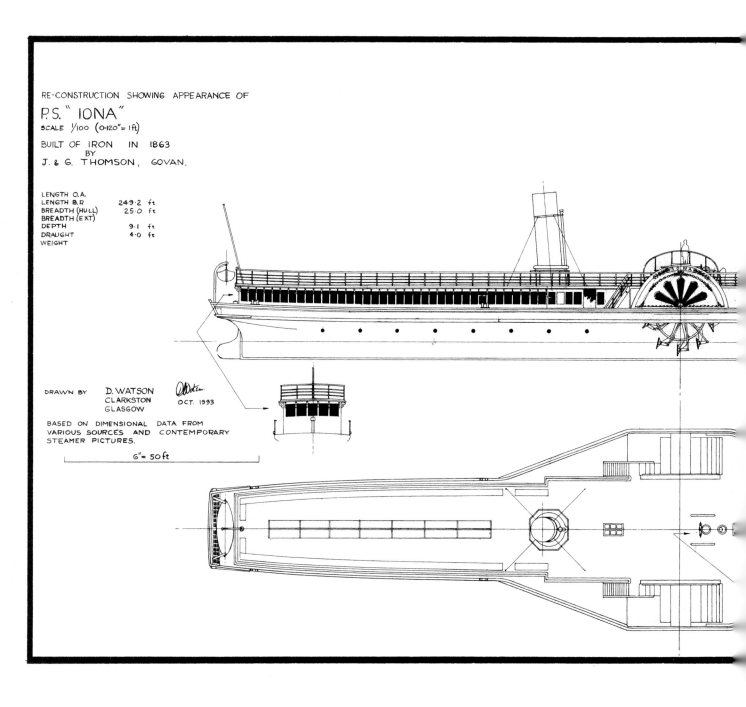

RE-CONSTRUCTION SHOWING APPEARANCE OF

P.S. " IONA "
SCALE 1/100 (0·120"= 1ft)

BUILT OF IRON IN 1863
BY
J. & G. THOMSON, GOVAN.

LENGTH O.A.
LENGTH B.P   249·2 ft
BREADTH (HULL)   25·0 ft
BREADTH (EXT)
DEPTH   9·1 ft
DRAUGHT   4·0 ft
WEIGHT

DRAWN BY   D. WATSON
            CLARKSTON   OCT. 1993
            GLASGOW

BASED ON DIMENSIONAL DATA FROM
VARIOUS SOURCES AND CONTEMPORARY
STEAMER PICTURES.

              6"= 50 ft

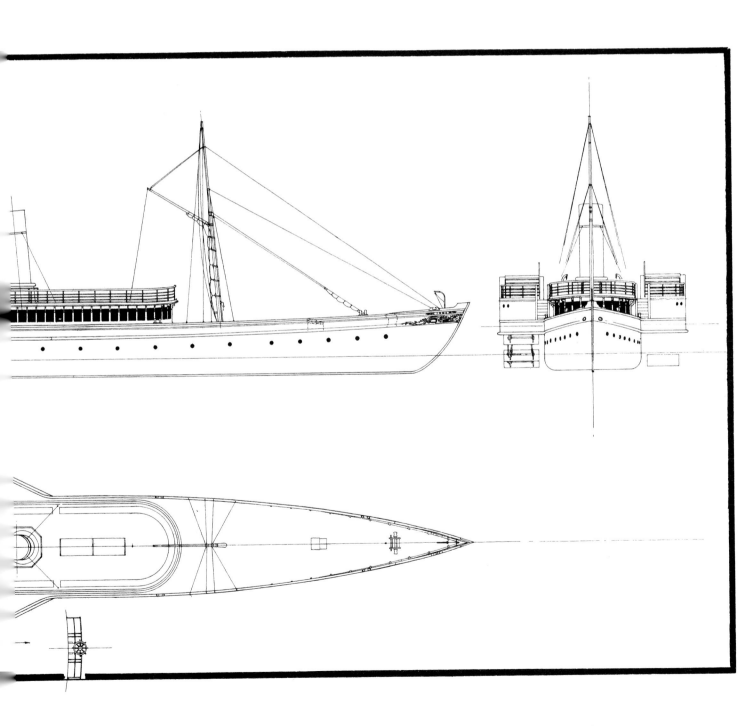

Builder:	J & G Thomson, Govan.	
Engine:	Oscillating, J & G Thomson.	
Boiler:	Horizontal.	**1864-1891**
	Haystack	**1891-1936**
Owner:	David Huchison & Co.	**1864-1879**
	David MacBrayne.	**1879-1905**
	David MacBrayne Ltd.	**1905-1923**
	David MacBrayne Ltd.	**1923-1928**
	D. MacBrayne (1928) Ltd. (Part of LMS)	**1928-1934**
	David MacBrayne Ltd.	**1934-1936**
	Arnot, Young & Co. (Shpbrkrs) Ltd.	**1936**
Captain:	McGowan, J. McGaw.	
Service:	Glasgow, Ardrishaig, Tarbert, Oban, Loch Long.	
End:	Laid up in 1935, and finally broken up at Dalmuir in 1936.	

THIS steamer, the last of the three ships named *Iona* built for David Huchison & Co.'s West coast services, was built in 1864, being launched on the 10th of May that year, and served for seventy-one years, being laid up in 1935, and finally broken up at Dalmuir in 1936. She replaced the second *Iona*, which had been sold to the Confederate States in 1863 for use as a blockade runner.

When built, she was almost a copy of her predecessor, but was slightly longer (by 11ft) and marginally broader (by 6"). Her deck saloons were those which had been removed from the earlier ship, as they were not wanted

on a blockade runner. The use of the existing deck saloons provided alleyways around the outside, as had been the case on the original ship.

The *Iona (III)*, like her earlier sisters, had rather squat funnels placed quite far apart, due to the use of horizontal, navy type boilers. In 1891, however, when her boilers were replaced for the second time, haystack boilers were fitted, and this enabled the aft funnel to be moved forward a short distance. At the same time the funnels were increased in height, and many people are of the opinion that these changes improved the appearance of the ship.

The draught of the *Iona* was reduced after completion of this refit.

In 1871 a bridge was added between the paddleboxes, and two years later, in 1873, at the same time as her first reboilering, steam steering gear, an engine telegraph, and a deck office positioned below the bridge, were added. The bridge was extended over the deck office in 1875, and it is thought that the awning behind the deck office was added at the same time, presumably to provide some degree of shelter at the deck office ticket window.

It was after the 1875 overhaul that the engines of the *Iona* were open to the public, a tradition which has been continued up until the present day in the famous 1947 paddle steamer *Waverley*.

An oil-gas lighting system was installed in 1880, along with an extra lifeboat mounted forward of the starboard paddle sponson. the lifeboat arrangement was again changed in 1891, when only two lifeboats were carried, mounted aft of the sponsons.

The *Titanic* disaster of 1912 caused some rethinking of ship lifeboat requirements, and in 1913 the *Iona* was fitted with four lifeboats, mounted fore and aft on both paddle boxes. It is thought that the life rafts positioned on top of the deck office awning were added at this time also.

The last noticeable change which seems to have been carried out on the *Iona*, was in 1918, when the forward deck saloon, during refurbishment, was lengthened by about ten feet.

During her career, the *Iona* has sailed at some time between Wemyss Bay, Greenock, Rothesay, Ardrishaig, and Tarbert, and at times served Lochgoilhead, Arrochar, and Oban.

She was a beautiful ship, and at her peak could carry up to 1400 passengers. Many people were sorry to see her being withdrawn from service in 1935.

Reproduced courtesy of The Scottish Maritime Museum.
The P.S. Iona 1864

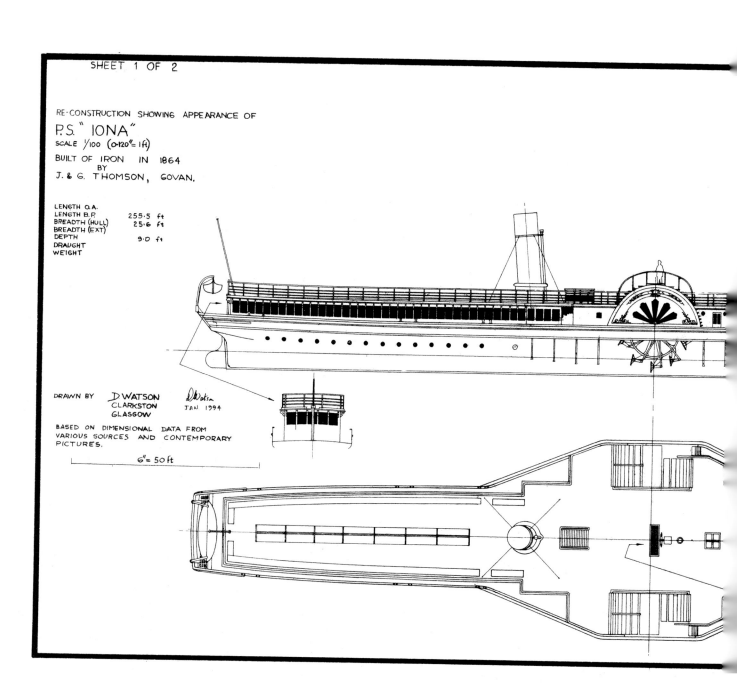

SHEET 1 OF 2

RE-CONSTRUCTION SHOWING APPEARANCE OF

P.S. "IONA"

SCALE 1/100 (0·120" = 1 ft)

BUILT OF IRON IN 1864
                    BY
J. & G. THOMSON, GOVAN.

LENGTH O.A.
LENGTH B.P.   255·5 ft
BREADTH (HULL)   25·6 ft
BREADTH (EXT)
DEPTH   9·0 ft
DRAUGHT
WEIGHT

DRAWN BY   D WATSON   D Watson
            CLARKSTON   JAN 1994
            GLASGOW

BASED ON DIMENSIONAL DATA FROM
VARIOUS SOURCES AND CONTEMPORARY
PICTURES.

6" = 50 ft

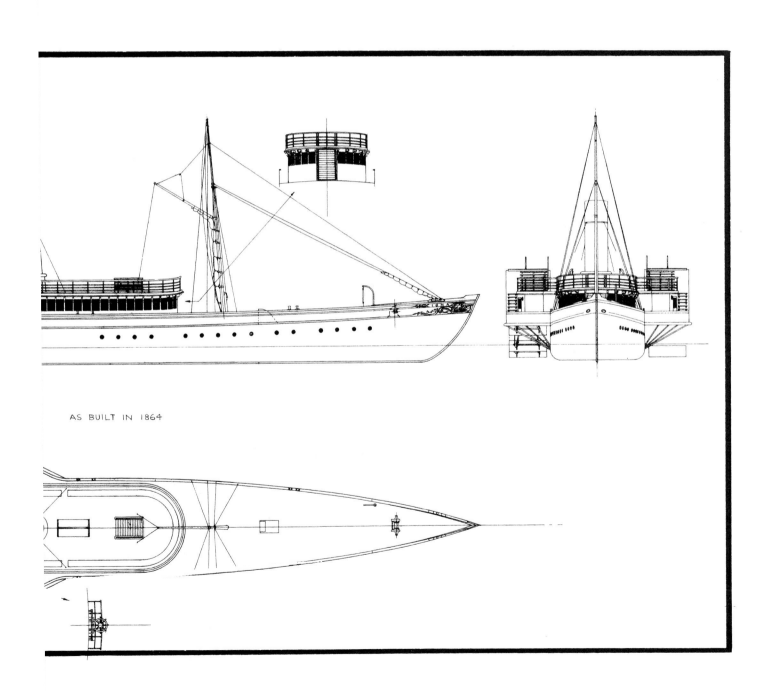

AS BUILT IN 1864

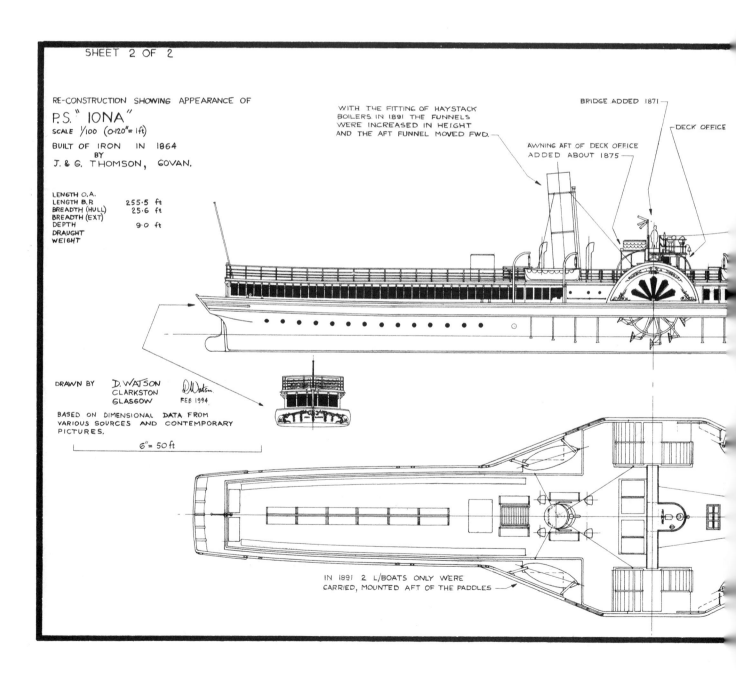

SHEET 2 OF 2

RE-CONSTRUCTION SHOWING APPEARANCE OF

P.S. " IONA "
SCALE 1/100 (0·120"= 1ft)
BUILT OF IRON IN 1864
BY
J. & G. THOMSON, GOVAN.

LENGTH O.A.
LENGTH B.R   255·5 ft
BREADTH (HULL)   25·6 ft
BREADTH (EXT)
DEPTH   9·0 ft
DRAUGHT
WEIGHT

WITH THE FITTING OF HAYSTACK
BOILERS IN 1891 THE FUNNELS
WERE INCREASED IN HEIGHT
AND THE AFT FUNNEL MOVED FWD.

BRIDGE ADDED 1871

DECK OFFICE

AWNING AFT OF DECK OFFICE
ADDED ABOUT 1875

DRAWN BY   D. WATSON
              CLARKSTON
              GLASGOW   FEB 1994

BASED ON DIMENSIONAL DATA FROM
VARIOUS SOURCES AND CONTEMPORARY
PICTURES.

6"= 50 ft

IN 1891 2 L/BOATS ONLY WERE
CARRIED, MOUNTED AFT OF THE PADDLES

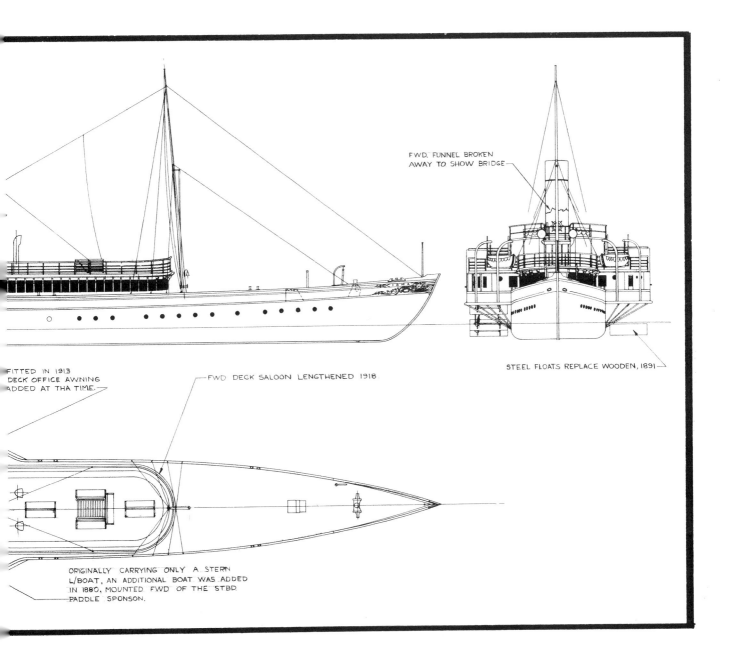

FWD. FUNNEL BROKEN
AWAY TO SHOW BRIDGE

STEEL FLOATS REPLACE WOODEN, 1891

FITTED IN 1913
DECK OFFICE AWNING
ADDED AT THA TIME.

FWD DECK SALOON LENGTHENED 1918

ORIGINALLY CARRYING ONLY A STERN
L/BOAT, AN ADDITIONAL BOAT WAS ADDED
IN 1880, MOUNTED FWD OF THE STBD
PADDLE SPONSON.

Builder:	Barclay Curle & Co., Whiteinch.	
Engine:	Single Diagonal 50" x 72" by Barclay Curle & Co.	
Boiler:	Haystack.	
Owner:	North British Steam Pkt. Co.	1884-1896
	Derry & Moville Steam Pkt. Co. Ltd.,	
	Londonderry.	1896-1898
	Glasgow Steamers Ltd. (W. Dawson Reid).	1898-1904
	Buchanan Steamers Ltd.	1904-1920
	Williamson-Buchanan Steamers Ltd.	1920-B.U.
Captain (1st):	D. McKinlay.	
Service:	Craigendorran, Rothesay, Clyde Coasts.	
End:	Broken up 1920.	

THIS was the last raised quarter deck steamer to be built for use on the Clyde, all subsequent ships having had deck saloons. In her day she must have been the fastest steamer on the Clyde, and with a mean speed of 17.5 knots, was able to hold her own against even the famous *Columba*. Her ability to maintain a good speed however, was to suffer badly, when in 1894, it was decided that her passenger accommodation would have to be upgraded, and deck saloons were added fore and aft. The forward deck saloon was a fairly short structure but its addition also necessitated a new companionway for access to the promenade deck above. At about the same time, or perhaps a short time later, a small 'office' was added underneath the bridge, and the pilot's wheel was relocated on the bridge on top of this 'office'.

Two years after these changes, in 1896, the *Jeanie Deans* was sold, and plied for Irish owners for two seasons, after which, in 1898 she again changed hands. As well as having new owners in 1898, she was also given a new name, being called *Duchess of York*. She sailed under her new name until, after lying idle for a season, she was bought in 1904 by her fourth owner, Buchanan Steamers Ltd., who re-named her once more, calling her *Isle of Cumbrae*. For the new owner the forward saloon was altered, being made slightly longer and with access at the front, the promenade deck forward companionway was changed, and the paddle box venting and decoration was re-designed.

In 1920 *Isle of Cumbrae* was taken over by Williamson-Buchanan Steamers Ltd., but was not operational. She was finally broken up in 1920.

Reproduced courtesy of The Mitchell Library, Glasgow City Libraries & Archives
The Jeanie Deans 1884

Reproduced courtesy of The Mitchell Library, Glasgow City Libraries & Archives
The P.S. Duchess of York (ex. Jeanie Deans 1884)

SHEET 1 OF 2

RE-CONSTRUCTION SHOWING APPEARANCE OF

P.S."JEANIE DEANS"/ (1884-1898)
"DUCHESS OF YORK"/(1898-1904)
"ISLE OF CUMBRAE"(1904-1920)

SCALE 1/100 (0·120"=1 Ft)

BUILT OF IRON & STEEL IN 1884
BY
BARCLAY   CURLE   C°
WHITEINCH

LENGTH O.A.
LENGTH B.P   210'
BREADTH (HULL)   20·1'
BREADTH (EXT)
DEPTH   7·6'
DRAUGHT
WEIGHT   271 TONS GROSS

6" = 50 ft

DRAWN BY   D. WATSON
                CLARKSTON
                GLASGOW   MAY 1991

        BASED ON DIMENSIONAL DATA FROM VARIOUS SOURCES,
        AND CONTEMPORARY STEAMER PICTURES.

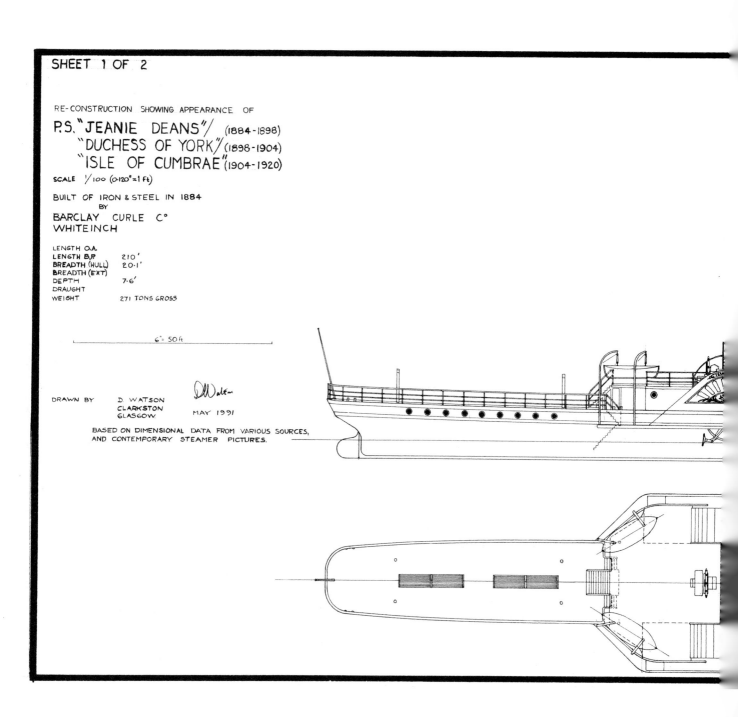

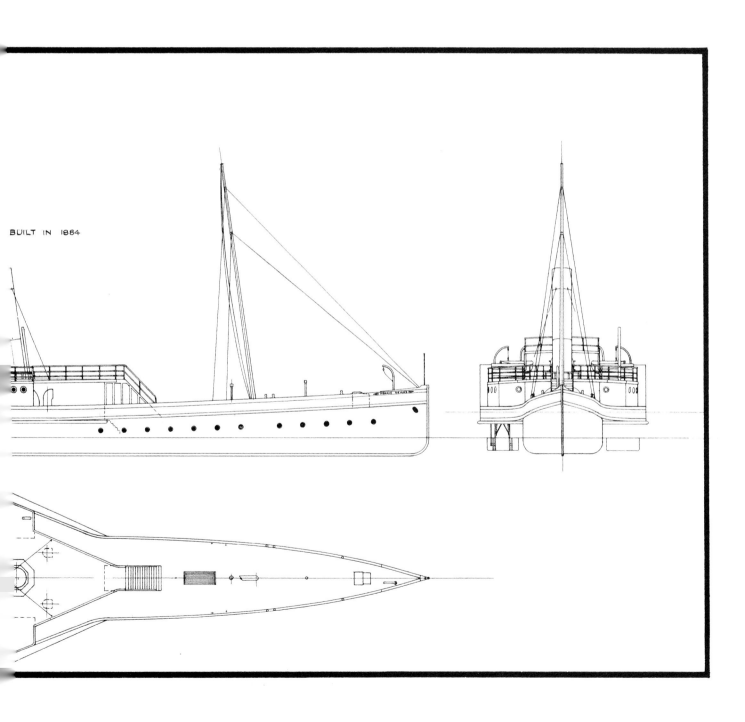

BUILT IN 1884

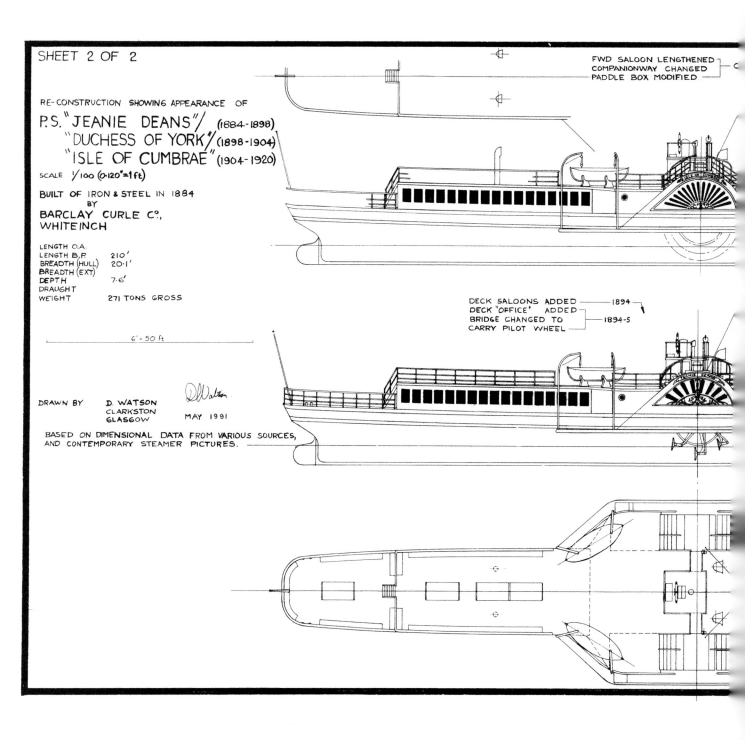

SHEET 2 OF 2

FWD SALOON LENGTHENED
COMPANIONWAY CHANGED
PADDLE BOX MODIFIED

RE-CONSTRUCTION SHOWING APPEARANCE OF
P.S. "JEANIE DEANS" (1884-1898)
    "DUCHESS OF YORK" (1898-1904)
    "ISLE OF CUMBRAE" (1904-1920)

SCALE 1/100 (0·120"=1ft)

BUILT OF IRON & STEEL IN 1884
              BY
BARCLAY CURLE C°,
WHITEINCH

LENGTH O.A.
LENGTH B.P.   210'
BREADTH (HULL)   20·1'
BREADTH (EXT)
DEPTH   7·6'
DRAUGHT
WEIGHT   271 TONS GROSS

6" = 50 ft

DECK SALOONS ADDED ———— 1894
DECK "OFFICE" ADDED ———
BRIDGE CHANGED TO   1894-5
CARRY PILOT WHEEL ————

DRAWN BY   D. WATSON
              CLARKSTON
              GLASGOW   MAY 1991

BASED ON DIMENSIONAL DATA FROM VARIOUS SOURCES,
AND CONTEMPORARY STEAMER PICTURES. ———

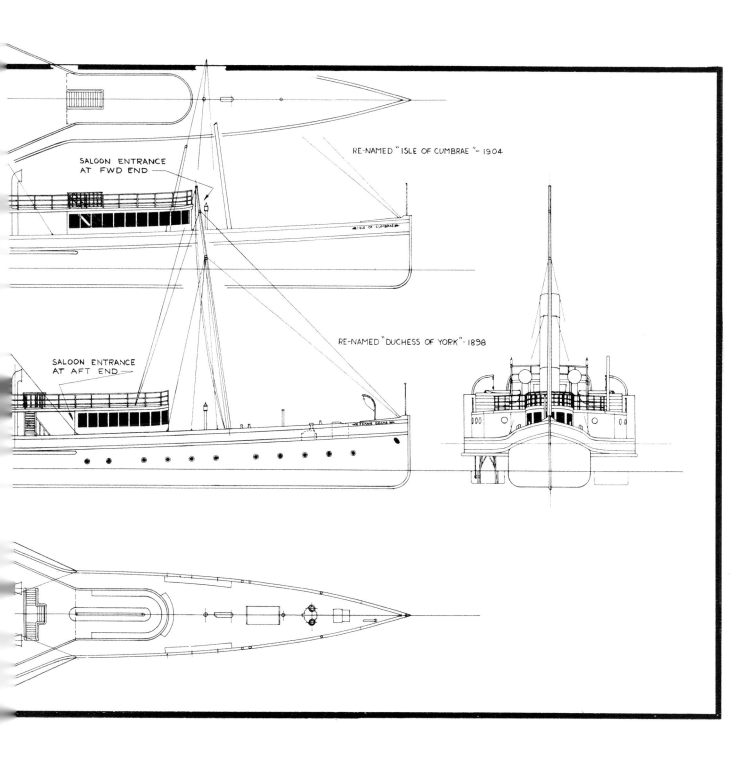

SALOON ENTRANCE
AT FWD END

RE-NAMED "ISLE OF CUMBRAE" - 1904

RE-NAMED "DUCHESS OF YORK" - 1898

SALOON ENTRANCE
AT AFT END

Builder:	**Fairfield Engineering & Ship Building Co. Ltd., Govan.**	
Engine:	**Fairfield Engineering & Ship Building Co. Ltd., Govan.**	
Boiler:	**Double Ended.**	
Owner:	**London North Eastern Railway.**	**1931-1948**
	British Rail.	**1948-1951**
	Caledonian Steam Pkt. Co.	**1951-1965**
	Coastal Steam Pkt. Co., London.	**1965-1967**
Captain (1st):	**Duncan Campbell.**	
Service:	**Craigendorran, Lochgoilhead, Arrochar.**	
End:	**Broken up 1967.**	

THE *Jeanie Deans* was built for the LNER which took over from the North British Railway in 1923 when the railways were re-grouped under the 1921 Railways act. She was the largest ship built to operate from Craigendorran, and was regarded as a 'flyer' being capable of steaming at 18.5 knots. To drive her she was equipped with a triple expansion three cylinder engine, and was the first Clyde steamer to have this type of engine fitted.

Licenced to carry 1,714 passengers, she served on the Lochgoil and Arrochar route, where she was an immediate success in her first season, the only criticism being about the falling of ash and soot on the passengers on the open deck. This fault was rectified in time for the second season, the funnels being heightened, the forward one by nine feet and the aft one by six feet, giving a slightly odd appearance to the ship. Another change completed in time for the 1932 season was the addition of a new deck shelter on the forward promenade deck, in order to provide more protection for passengers in the event of bad weather.

In 1939 the start of the war meant that many changes were to take place, and the *Jeanie Deans*, like many of her contemporaries, was requisitioned by the Admiralty and served firstly as a minesweeper and later as an escort, and then an anti-aircraft ship.

When the war was over the *Jeanie Deans* returned to the Clyde and was completely reconditioned by A J Inglis, before taking up her old duties again. She was transformed! A new, longer forward deck shelter, or saloon, was fitted, above which was built a new bridge, wheelhouse and captain's cabin. The old unequal height funnels were replaced by new eliptical funnels of equal height and a deck shelter was added aft of the paddle boxes. This aft deck shelter was provided with a passenger deck space on top, and the four lifeboats, originally positioned on the paddle sponsons, were replaced by new lifeboats and davits located on boat decks on top of the new forward and aft deck houses.

A main mast which passed through the new aft deck shelter was added, and the plating up to main deck level at the stern, which had been done for her wartime service, was retained.

In 1957 she was converted to burn oil instead of coal, and radar was added in 1960.

Jeanie Deans was withdrawn from Clyde service in 1965, and was sold to a new owner, the Coastal Steam Packet Co. Ltd., who intended to use her on the River Thames. Her new owner re-named her *Queen of the South*. She was however, dogged by breakdowns and was laid up at the end of the 1966 season. Repair work was carried out, and in 1967, after major boiler work and interior refurbishment, she was again plying on the Thames. This, alas, was not destined to last for long, as further breakdowns led to her being withdrawn and sold for breaking up at the end of 1967.

Reproduced courtesy of The Mitchell Library, Glasgow City Libraries & Archives
The P.S. Jeanie Deans 1931

Reproduced courtesy of The Mitchell Library, Glasgow City Libraries & Archives
The P.S. Jeanie Deans 1931

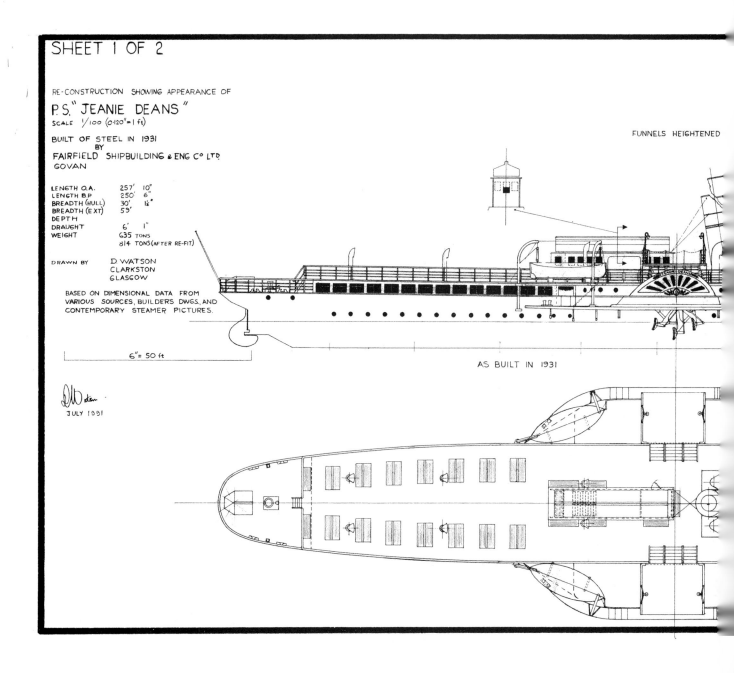

SHEET 1 OF 2

RE-CONSTRUCTION SHOWING APPEARANCE OF

P.S. "JEANIE DEANS"
SCALE 1/100 (0.120"= 1 ft)

BUILT OF STEEL IN 1931
BY
FAIRFIELD SHIPBUILDING & ENG C° LTD
GOVAN

LENGTH O.A.   257' 10"
LENGTH B.P   250' 6"
BREADTH (HULL)   30' 1½"
BREADTH (EXT)   59'
DEPTH
DRAUGHT   6' 1"
WEIGHT   635 TONS
                 814 TONS (AFTER RE-FIT)

DRAWN BY   D WATSON
              CLARKSTON
              GLASGOW

BASED ON DIMENSIONAL DATA FROM
VARIOUS SOURCES, BUILDERS DWGS, AND
CONTEMPORARY STEAMER PICTURES.

6"= 50 ft

JULY 1931

FUNNELS HEIGHTENED

AS BUILT IN 1931

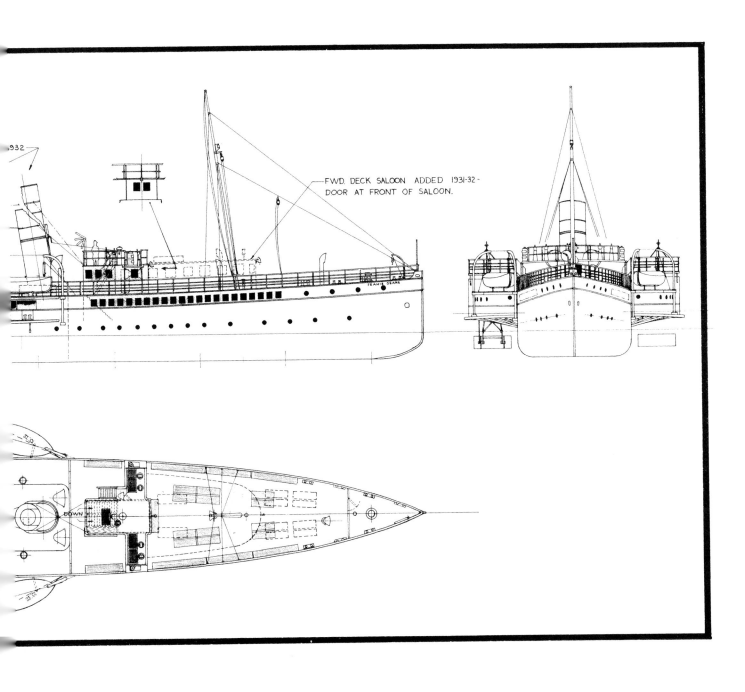

FWD. DECK SALOON ADDED 1931-32 -
DOOR AT FRONT OF SALOON.

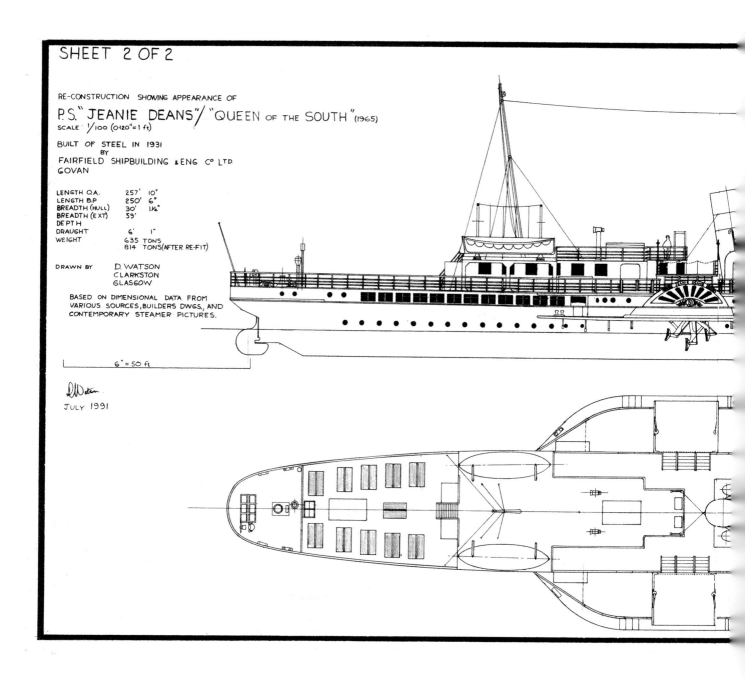

SHEET 2 OF 2

RE-CONSTRUCTION SHOWING APPEARANCE OF

P.S. "JEANIE DEANS"/ "QUEEN OF THE SOUTH" (1965)
SCALE 1/100 (0.120"=1 ft)

BUILT OF STEEL IN 1931
            BY
FAIRFIELD SHIPBUILDING & ENG C° LTD
GOVAN

LENGTH O.A.   257' 10"
LENGTH B.P   250' 6"
BREADTH (HULL)   30' 1¼"
BREADTH (EXT)   59'
DEPTH
DRAUGHT   6' 1"
WEIGHT   635 TONS
               814 TONS (AFTER RE-FIT)

DRAWN BY   D. WATSON
            CLARKSTON
            GLASGOW

       BASED ON DIMENSIONAL DATA FROM
       VARIOUS SOURCES, BUILDERS DWGS., AND
       CONTEMPORARY STEAMER PICTURES.

            6" = 50 ft

JULY 1991

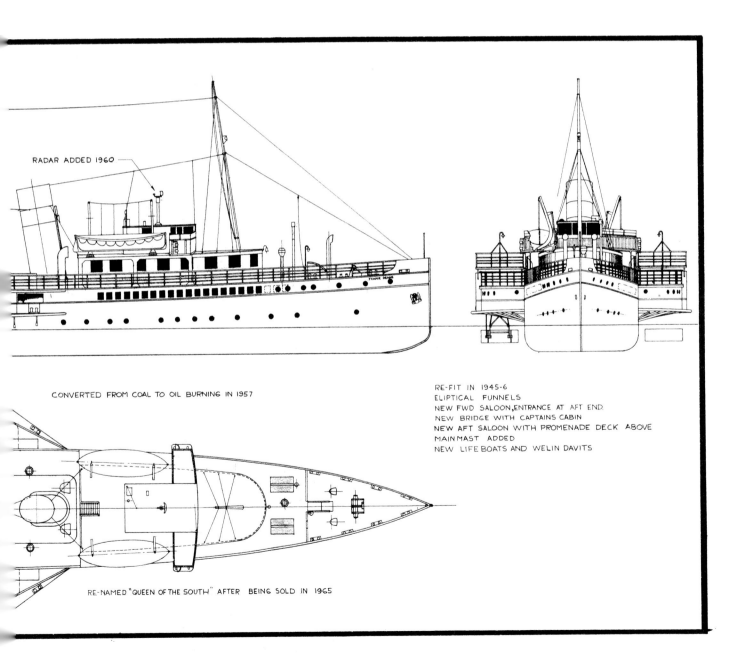

RADAR ADDED 1960

CONVERTED FROM COAL TO OIL BURNING IN 1957

RE-FIT IN 1945-6
ELIPTICAL FUNNELS
NEW FWD SALOON, ENTRANCE AT AFT END.
NEW BRIDGE WITH CAPTAINS CABIN
NEW AFT SALOON WITH PROMENADE DECK ABOVE
MAINMAST ADDED
NEW LIFE BOATS AND WELIN DAVITS

RE-NAMED "QUEEN OF THE SOUTH" AFTER BEING SOLD IN 1965

Builder:	Denny Brothers.	
Engine:	Smith & Rodger.	
Boiler:	Unknown.	
Owner:	Dumbarton Steamboat Co.	**1845-1852**
	Glasgow, Paisley & Greenock RLY (CAL RLY).	**1852-1854**
	Henry Nicholls, Eastham.	**1854-1856**
	William Hillian, Eastham.	**1856-1862**
	James Whitehead, Preston.	**1862-1864**
	Messrs Allsup.	**1864**
Captain:	R. Long.	
Service:	Dumbarton, Helensburgh, Glasgow.	
End:	Broken up 1864.	

THE paddle steamer *Loch Lomond* was the first ship to be built by the new marine architects and shipbuilding company of Denny Brothers, which was formed in 1844 by William Denny, with his brothers Peter and Alexander as partners.

Launched in 1845, of flush deck design, the *Loch Lomond* was an iron, clinker built, flush riveted ship, ordered by the Dumbarton Steamboat Co. She was stationed on the Glasgow to Dumbarton route while being worked by the Dumbarton Steamboat.Co., but may have served other ports from time to time.

In 1852 it seems she was sold to the Glasgow, Paisley, and Greenock Railway Co., who operated steamers connecting with their trains, but who, in turn, sold her again in 1854 when they gave up steamer operation. She spent the remaining part of her life in England before being finally broken up in 1864 by Messrs Allsup.

The P.S. Loch Lomond 1845

RE-CONSTRUCTION SHOWING APPEARANCE OF

P.S. " LOCH LOMOND "

SCALE 1/100 (0·120" = 1ft)

BUILT OF **IRON** IN 1845
BY
Wm. DENNY & BROTHERS
DUMBARTON.

LENGTH O.A.	
LENGTH B.P.	126'
BREADTH (HULL)	16' - 9"
BREADTH (EXT)	
DEPTH	6' - 7"
DRAUGHT	
WEIGHT	95 TONS

DRAWN BY   D. WATSON   *D.Watson.*
             CLARKSTON   OCT. 1992.
             GLASGOW

BASED ON DIMENSIONAL DATA FROM VARIOUS SOURCES,
CONTEMPORARY STEAMER PICTURES AND A COPY OF
BUILDERS DRAWING

6" = 50 ft

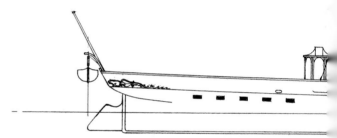

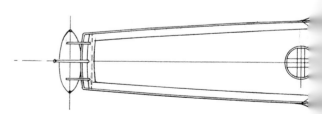

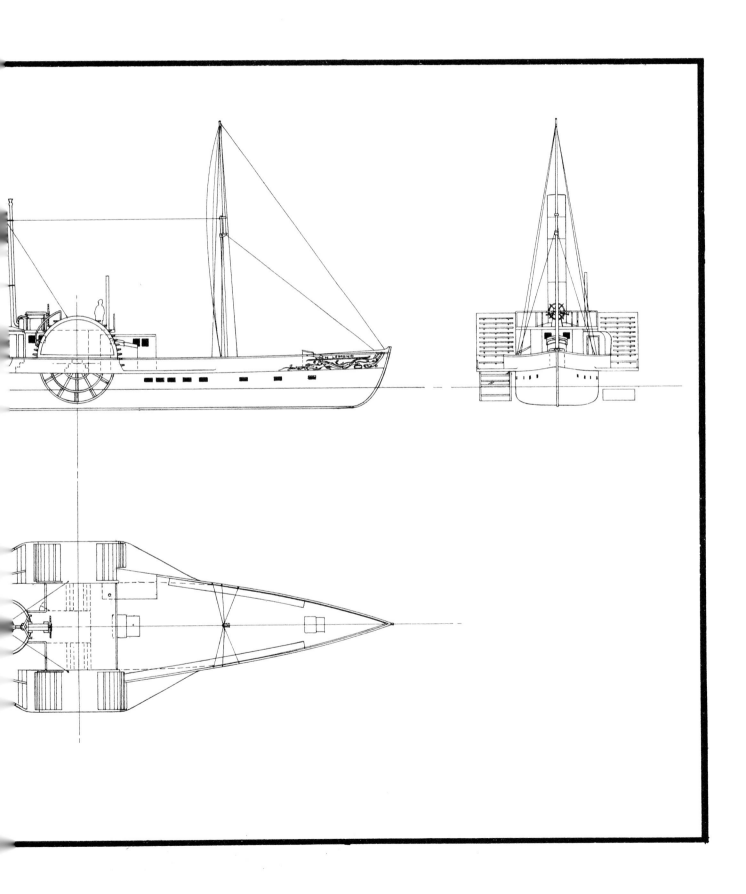

1816

MARION

Builder:	**Archibald McLachlan, Dumbarton.**
Engine:	**David Napier.**
Boiler:	**Unknown.**
Owner:	**David Napier, - McMurrich.**　　　**1816-1832**
Captain:	**Unknown.**
Service:	**Glasgow - Greenock, then Loch Lomond.**
End:	**Wrecked in River Leven, 1832.**

NAMED after David Napier's wife, the PS *Marion* was a neat little paddle steamer, having one main saloon aft of the paddle wheels, and a small cabin forward. She served on Loch Lomond for 15 years, after spending her first year on the Glasgow - Greenock run. She was the first steamer to ply on Loch Lomond, and was put there by David Napier when he was opening up an alternative route to Inveraray.

As well as being the first steamboat to serve on Loch Lomond, the PS *Marion* can claim to have sailed further up the River Clyde than any other steamer, having gone beyond the site of TB Seath's Rutherglen yard to call at Dalmarnock.

She was sold in 1832, but while being taken down the River Leven towards Dumbarton for her new owners, she was stranded, and unfortunately became a total loss.

Fred M. Walker's book "Song of the Clyde" reproduces a painting of the *Marion*.

Reproduced courtesy of The Mitchell Library, Glasgow City Libraries & Archives

The P.S. Marion 1816

RE-CONSTRUCTION SHOWING POSSIBLE APPEARANCE OF

P.S. "MARION"

SCALE ¹⁄₁₀₀ (0.120" = 1 ft.

BUILT OF WOOD IN 1816
                BY
ARCHIBALD McLACHLAN,
DUMBARTON,

LENGTH O.A.   85' (72' KEEL)
LENGTH B.P.   60'
BREADTH (HULL)   13'
BREADTH (EXT)
DEPTH
DRAUGHT   2'- 9"
WEIGHT   57 TONS GROSS

DRAWN BY   D. WATSON
                CLARKSTON   OCT. 1991
                GLASGOW

        BASED ON DIMENSIONAL DATA FROM VARIOUS
        SOURCES, AND CONTEMPORARY STEAMER PICTURES.

        ⊢————————— 6" = 50 ft —————————⊣

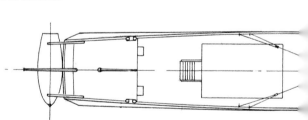

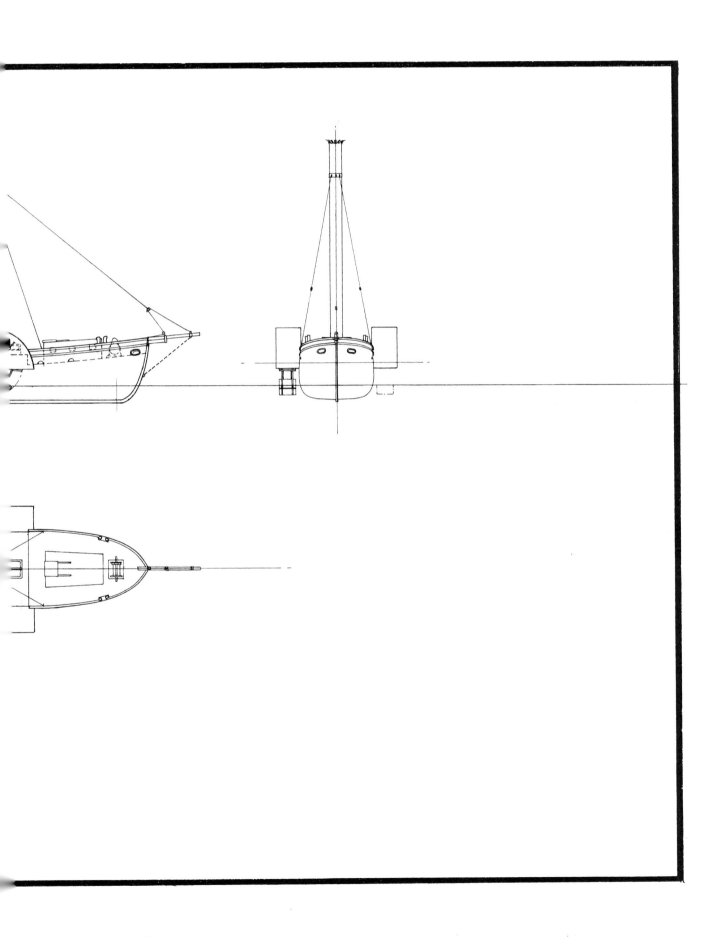

Builder:	**Caird & Co., Greenock.**	
Engine:	**Caird & Co., Greenock.**	
Boiler:	**Haystack.**	
Owner:	**W. F. Johnstone, Neil McGill.**	**1854-1861**
Captain:	**Neil McGill.**	
Service:	**Glasgow, Rothesay, Ardrishaig.**	
End:	**Sold to India 1860.**	

THIS was the third *Rothesay Castle* to sail the waters of the River Clyde. Five ships of that name were built, but of these only this one, known at the time as *Cairds Rothesay Castle*, and her successor (built by William Simons) were noted for their ability to show a good turn of speed. This *Rothesay Castle* was a flush decked steamer of very pleasing appearance, and is said to have had an abundance of gold decoration on her hull and paddle boxes.

After only one season on the Glasgow-Rothesay run she was transferred to the Glasgow-Ardrishaig service, but was back on the Rothesay service in 1856.

At the end on 1860 it was announced that she was being sold to an owner in India. Her engines were taken out and shipped out separately, her paddle boxes were removed, her hull given internal stiffening, and she was rigged out as a three masted schooner.

She set sail for India, but heading southwards from the Clyde bad weather drove her repeatedly into Irish ports, till eventually she returned to the Clyde, being towed into Greenock at the end of June in 1861. This was not the end of her career, as she was dismantled and sent out to India in pieces, there to be reassembled for duty on some Indian river.

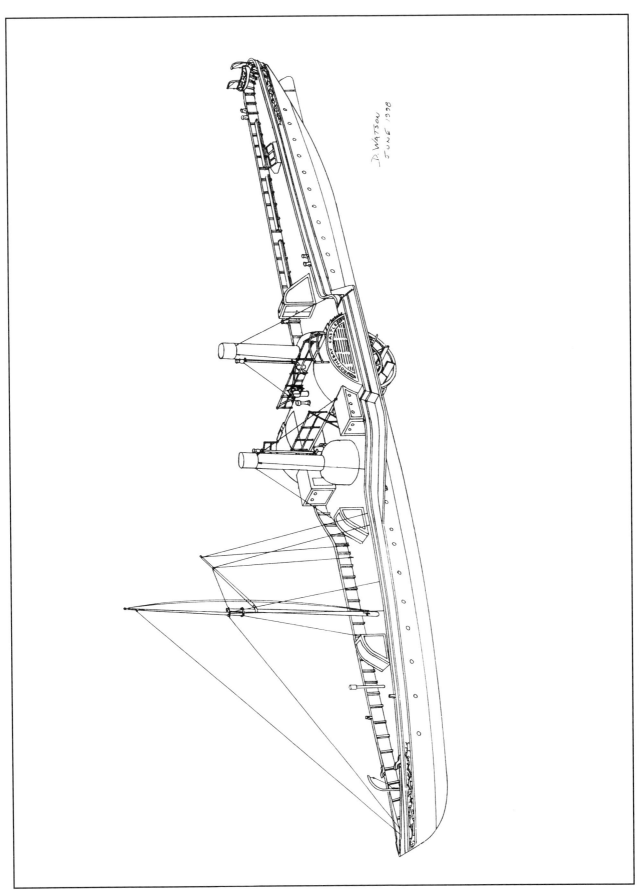

The P.S. Rothesay Castle 1854 – Author's drawing

RE-CONSTRUCTION SHOWING POSSIBLE APPEARANCE OF

P. S. "ROTHESAY   CASTLE"
SCALE 1/100 (0·120"= 1 ft)

BUILT OF IRON IN 1854
                    BY
CAIRD & C°
GREENOCK.

LENGTH O.A.
LENGTH B.P   181'- 10"
BREADTH (HULL)   17' - 10"
BREADTH (EXT)
DEPTH   8' - 1"
DRAUGHT
WEIGHT   112·66 TONS

                  6"= 50 ft

DRAWN BY   D. WATSON
              CLARKSTON
              GLASGOW   JULY 1990

        BASED ON DIMENSIONAL DATA FROM VARIOUS SOURCES, AND
        CONTEMPORARY STEAMER PICTURES

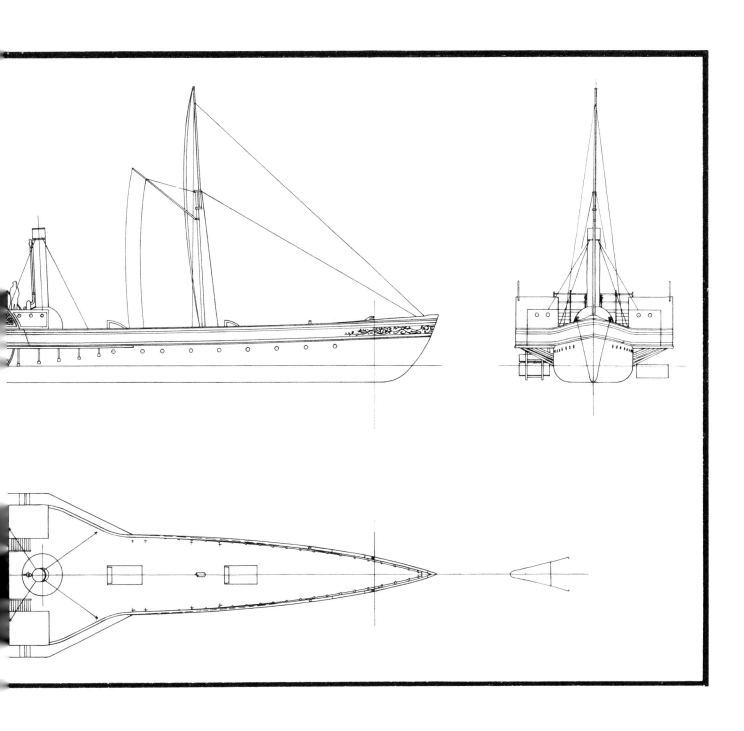

Builder:	**William Simons & Co., Renfrew.**	
Engine:	**William Simons & Co.**	
Boiler:	**Haystack.**	
Owner:	**A. Watson.**	**1861-1863**
	Confederate States.	**1863-**
Captain:	**M. Campbell.**	
Service:	**Glasgow, Rothesay.**	
End:	**Sold to Confederate States 1863.**	

THE *Rothesay Castle* of 1861, the fourth steamer of that name, was a sleek looking, flush decked ship, with a straight stem and two funnels. She was well known for her speed, and often raced with her contemporaries on her Glasgow to Rothesay run.

It is likely that her ability to show a good turn of speed made her attractive to the agents for the Confederate States, and consequently she was sold in 1863 for use as a blockade runner. She seems to have been very succesful in avoiding the Federal States blockade ships, for she was never captured, and after the war she was to be found plying on the Canadian Lakes, under the name of *Southern Belle*.

Reproduced courtesy of The Mitchell Library, Glasgow City Libraries & Archives
The P.S. Rothesay Castle 1861

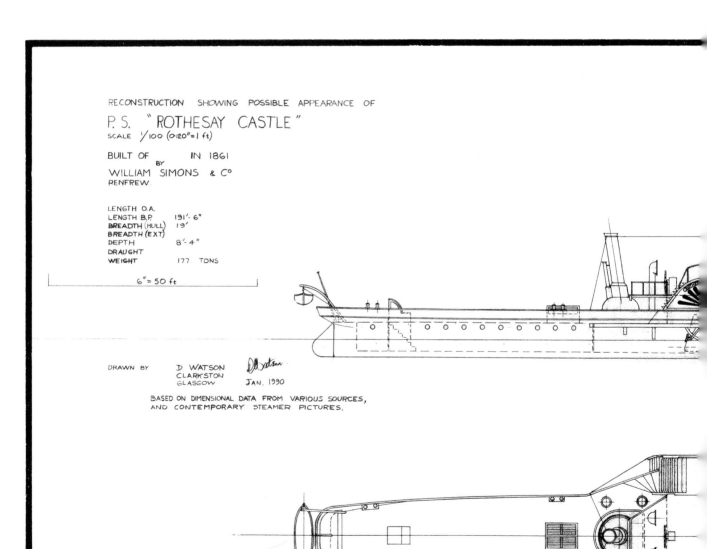

RECONSTRUCTION SHOWING POSSIBLE APPEARANCE OF

P. S. "ROTHESAY CASTLE"
SCALE 1/100 (0.120"=1 ft)

BUILT OF   IN 1861
              BY
WILLIAM SIMONS & C°
RENFREW.

LENGTH O.A.
LENGTH B.P.   191'- 6"
BREADTH (HULL)   19'
BREADTH (EXT)
DEPTH   8'- 4"
DRAUGHT
WEIGHT   177 TONS

6" = 50 ft

DRAWN BY   D WATSON
                  CLARKSTON
                  GLASGOW   JAN. 1990

BASED ON DIMENSIONAL DATA FROM VARIOUS SOURCES,
AND CONTEMPORARY STEAMER PICTURES.

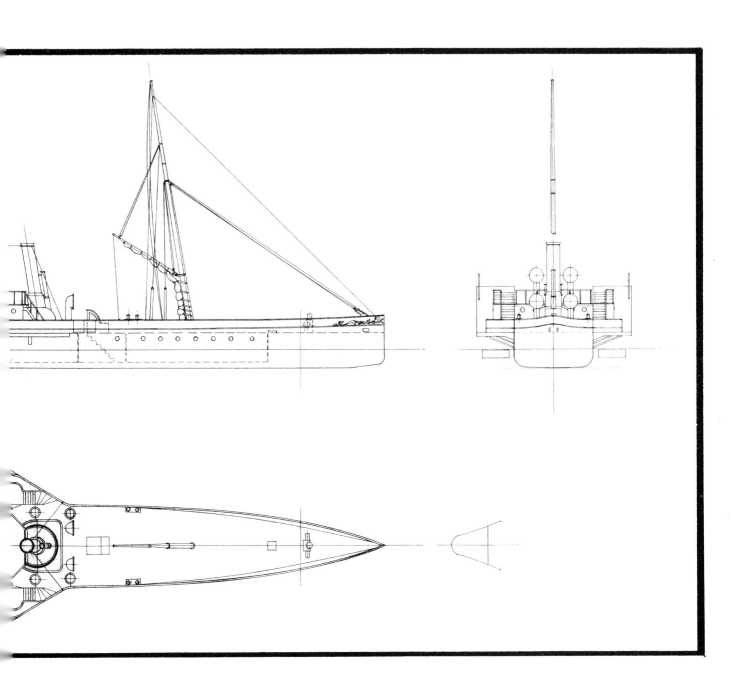

SECTION 2

PADDLE STEAMER SETS

Paddle Steamers which carry the same name

Albion: 1816, 1834, 18??, 1844, 1859, 1860, 1900.
Caledonia: 1815, 1826, 1840, 1844, 1856, 1889, 1934.
Chancellor: 1853, 1864, 1880.
City of Glasgow: 1822, 1835.
Clyde: 1813, 1832, 1841, 1851.
Comet: 1812, 1821, 189?.
Duke of Argyle-Argyll: 1814, 1852, 1873.

Eagle: 1835, 1852, 1864, 1910.
Edinburgh Castle: 1821, 1835, 1844, 1879.
Inveraray Castle: 1814, 1820, 1839.
Iona: 1855, 1863, 1864.
Jeanie Deans: 1884, 1931.
Loch Lomond: 1836, 1845, 1867.
Rothesay Castle: 1816, 1837, 1854, 1861, 1865.

PADDLE STEAMERS NAMED
ALBION

1st	1816 - ?		2nd	1834 - ?
3rd	18?? - ?		4th	1844 - ?
5th	1859 - ?		6th	1860 - ?
7th	1900 - ?			

1st 1816.
See drawing and separate notes.

2nd 1834.
This *Albion*, which sailed between Glasgow and Arran, with calls at Greenock, Largs, Millport, and Ardossan, is another ship the history of which is lost. James Williamson in his book tells us that she was built of wood, but the builder is not known, although a length of 115 feet 5 ins. and a beam of 16 feet 3 ins. is quoted. Her life and fate are unknown.

3rd 18??, 4th 1844
The records of the Strathclyde Regional Archives quote a steamer named *Albion*, built at an unknown date, probably by Tod & McGregor, of 145 feet length and 21 feet 3 ins. beam. There is also a steamer listed, named *Albion*, built in 1844 by Tod & McGregor operating on the Glasgow – Stranraer run, which has two sets of dimensions, one of which is the same as the first steamer listed. Little seems to be known about these ships, but it may be that these two records refer to the same vessel.

5th 1859
The Strathclyde Regional Archives list an *Albion* paddle steamer, built by Tod & McGregor in 1859. Yard No. 94 is all the information carried in the records about this ship.

6th 1860.
According to the Stathclyde Regional Archives, Tod & McGregor also built a paddle steamer named *Albion* in 1860, for the Stranraer Steamboat Co. This ship was 165 feet long by 24 feet beam.

7th 1900.
The *Albion* of 1900 was originally built in 1866 as the *Prince of Wales* by Aiken & Mansell.

Further research into steamers named *Albion* could no doubt reveal much more information.

PADDLE STEAMERS NAMED
CALEDONIA

1st	1815 - 1841		2nd	1826 - ?
3rd	1840 - ?		4th	1844 - ?
5th	1856 - ?		6th	1188 - 1933
7th	1934 - 1980			

1st 1815
See drawing and separate notes.

2nd 1826
After the first *Caledonia* had gone off to the Thames and eventually to Denmark in 1819, the second ship of the name was built by W. Denny, at Dumbarton. Little is known about this ship, other than that she was 84 feet long by 14 feet beam, and that she plied on the Greenock, Gourock, and Helensburgh run. Her career and final end is unknown.

3rd 1840
This ship, being a trans-Atlantic steamer built for the Cunard Co., does not really belong in the class of vessel covered in this presentation, but has been included only as one of the Clyde built paddle steamers named *Caledonia*. She was built by Charles Wood at Dumbarton.

4th 1844
Built of iron by Smith & Rodger, Govan, this steamer served Kilmun and the Holy Loch. Her history and final end is unknown, but it is said that she was similar in design to a contemporary steamer, the *Koh-I-Noor*.

5th 1856
Other than it being recorded that there was a ship named *Caledonia* built at this time, the

writer has no information about this vessel.

6th 1889
See drawing and separate notes.

7th 1934
See drawing and separate notes.

PADDLE STEAMERS NAMED
CHANCELLOR

1st   1853 - 1863   2nd   1864 - 1880
3rd   1880 - 1919,
then renamed
Shandon till 1893,
then renamed
Daniel Adamson till 1895

See drawing and separate notes for each of the three steamers named *Chancellor*.

PADDLE STEAMERS NAMED
CITY OF GLASGOW

1st   1822 - 18??   2nd   1835 - 18??

1st 1822
See drawing and separate notes.

2nd 1835
Being 156 feet in length and 24 feet 4 ins., in beam, this *City of Glasgow* was one of the biggest steamers in its day. The builder was John Wood of Port Glasgow, and she plied between Glasgow, The Isle of Man and Liverpool. She carried two masts and a bowsprit, and had one funnel. How long she sailed for, or her final fate is not known, but she was still operating in 1841.

PADDLE STEAMERS NAMED
CLYDE

1st   1813 - 1828   2nd   1832 - ?
3rd   1841 - 1865   4th   1851 - 1912

1st 1813
See drawing and separate notes.

2nd 1832
The second paddle steamer named *Clyde* was not a Clyde coast or west of Scotland steamer, but was a sea-going ship owned by G & J Burns, and traded between Glasgow and Liverpool. She is recorded as being fitted with one of the first steeple engines built by David Napier. How long this ship operated, or what her end was, is not known.

3rd 1841
This was an ocean-going paddle ship built of wood by Robert Duncan & Co. of Greenock, and was 213 feet long between perpendiculars. She was equipped with side lever engines produced by Caird & Co., Greenock, and had paddle wheels of thirty feet diameter. She was broken up in 1865.

4th 1851
The fourth paddle ship was the well known tug *Clyde*, the engines of which can still be seen at Renfrew on the Low Green, just next to the Renfrew ferry. She was built by   A & J Ingles Ltd., as was her two side lever engines, for the Clyde Navigation Trust, who employed her until 1912, a total of 61 years.

PADDLE STEAMERS NAMED
COMET

1st   1812 - 1820   2nd   1821 - 1825
3rd   189? - ?

1st 1812

See drawing and separate notes.

2nd 1821

After the loss of the first *Comet* in 1820, Henry Bell lost little time in encouraging, with assistance from others, the building of another steamer, which was also named *Comet* in honour of him and his first steamer.

The second *Comet*, built by James Lang of Dumbarton, was larger and had a more powerful engine than the first. She plied the same west coast route, and when the Caledonian Canal was opened to Inverness in 1822, she sailed to that town, instead of terminating her journey from Glasgow at Fort William.

Her career ended, however, in October 1825, on her return to Glasgow from her Inverness run, when she was delayed at the Crinan Canal basin at Ardrishaig, making her arrival at the Clyde late at night. In the darkness she was struck by the steamship *Ayr*, just off Gourock, and sank in about three minutes, with the loss of many passenger and crew lives.

The wreck of the *Comet* was raised in the following July, after which her engine was removed and she was converted to sail. She continued her life as the schooner *Anne* until 1876 when she was finally broken up.

3rd 189?

A third paddle steamer named *Comet* appeared in the 1880's, running short trips to Rothesay. This litlle ship had one funnel and a clipper bow.

PADDLE STEAMERS NAMED
DUKE OF ARGYLE
or *ARGYLL*

1st	**1814 - ?**	**2nd**	**1852 - 1858**
3rd	**1873 - 1905**		

1st 1814

See drawing and separate notes.

2nd 1852

The 1852 ship was built of iron by Scott & Sinclair Co., of Greenock, for trade to Lochfyne. She was lenghtened in 1855, and in 1857 became part of the David Huchison fleet. At the beginning of 1858 she sank off Mull, was raised and beached for examination, but was finally broken up in that year.

3rd 1873

This steamer was built at Port Glasgow, and was a cross channel steamer sailing between Glasgow and Dublin, for the Dublin & Glasgow Sailing & Steam Packet Co. She was scrapped in 1905.

PADDLE STEAMERS NAMED
EAGLE

1st	**1835 - 18??**	**2nd**	**1852 - 1862,** then renamed *Jeanette* in the Confederate States of America
3rd	**1864 - 1899**	**4th**	**1910 - 1946**

1st 1835

There is a record of a steamer, built by R. Steele & Co., Greenock, but no details are known to the writer.

2nd 1852

See drawing and separate notes.

3rd 1864

See drawing and separate notes.

4th 1910

See drawing and separate notes.

PADDLE STEAMERS NAMED
EDINBURGH CASTLE

1st   1821 - 18??   2nd   1835 - 1852
3rd   1844 - 1875,   4th   1879 - 1913
then renamed
Glengarry

1st 1821

The 1821 *Edinburgh Castle* was built at Port Glasgow, and operated on the east coast until, in 1849, she went to the Jersey Steam Navigation Co., for whom she sailed until 1854.

2nd 1835

Built of wood by Hunter & Dow, Glasgow, for the Castle Steam Packet Co., this steamer was sold in 1838 to a new owner in Rye, and in 1843 was resold to the South Western Steam Packet Co., which operated ships from Southampton. She was eventually sunk in 1852.

3rd 1844

See drawing and separate notes.

4th 1879

See drawing and separate notes.

PADDLE STEAMERS NAMED
INVERARAY CASTLE

1st   1814 - 19??   2nd   1820 - 1836
3rd   1839 - 1896

1st 1814

This steamer was built of wood by John Wood of Port Glasgow, and traded between Glasgow and Loch Fyne. She was 84 feet long with a beam of 17 feet, and was the largest steamer built on the Clyde up to that time. Again, the history and life of this ship is unknown.

2nd 1820

See drawing and separate notes.

3rd 1839

See drawing and separate notes.

PADDLE STEAMERS NAMED
IONA

1st   1855 - 1862   2nd   1863 - 1864
3rd   1864 - 1836

See drawing and separate notes for each of the three steamers named *Iona*.

PADDLE STEAMERS NAMED
JEANIE DEANS

1st 1884 - 1898,   2nd 1931 - 1965,
then renamed   then renamed
Duchess of York   *Queen of the*
till 1904, then   *South*
renamed *Isle*
of Cumbrae

See drawing and separate notes for each of the two steamers named *Jeanie Deans.*

PADDLE STEAMERS NAMED
LOCH LOMOND

1st   1836 - ?   2nd   1845 - 1864
3rd   1867 - 18??

1st 1836

This steamer was an iron, flush rivetted clinker built ship, from the yard of David Napier, who also supplied the engine, and who operated her on Loch Lomond. It is though that when built, she was flush decked, had two masts, a funnel located just aft of the sponsons, a standing bowsprit with a figurehead, and a square stern. Her aft mast was removed in 1851, and it seems that a raised quarter deck may have been added about 1846 when she passed into the ownership of a Fort William man, Mr Ainslie, who renamed her *Glencoe,* and sailed her on the Caledonian Canal. In 1849 she was again renamed, being called *Curlew,* when she became part of the G. & J. Burns fleet, until 1851 when David Huchison became her owner. After two years being laid up, she was sold in 1855 to Liverpool owners, and was eventually broken up in 1862

2nd 1845

See drawing and separate notes.

3rd 1867

Built by Denny Brothers of Dumbarton, the third *Loch Lomond* was an Iron flush decker steamer 120 feet long with a beam of 16.8 feet, which plied between Glasgow and Dumbarton. Peter Denny operated her on this route until 1869, but what happened to her after that is unknown.

PADDLE STEAMERS NAMED
ROTHESAY CASTLE

1st   1816 - 1831   2nd   1837 - 1853
3rd   1854 - 1861   4th   1861 - 1863
5th   1865 - 18??

1st 1816

The first *Rothesay Castle* was a wooden steamer built at Dumbarton by Archibald McLachlan, where William Denny was the yard manager prior to taking over McLachlan's business in 1818. The vessels single cylinder engine was produced by L. McArthur & Co.

As built she was 92 feet 11 ins. long, 16 feet 11 in. wide, had a depth of 8 feet 1 ins. and a gross tonnage of 74.4. She was launched in April 1816, and is reported to have achieved a speed of about 12 knots. With her single cylinder engine it is likely that she had one boiler and therefore only one funnel, other than that, however, her appearance is unknown.

She was built for the owners of the "Castle" boats, who originally held each ship as a separate company, until 1832 when the Castle Steam Packet Co., was formed. In March 1821 she was re-engined and lenghened, being then 98 feet long, with her depth increased to 9 feet 2.5 ins.

The Glasgow - Rothesay service was the route plied by the *Rothesay Castle,* and then later she also sailed from Glasgow to Ardrishaig and Inveraray.

In 1830 she was sold to new owners in Liverpool, and it was while in their service that she tragically met her end. On the morning of the 17th of August 1831 the *Rothesay Castle* carrying many passengers, left Liverpool bound for Beaumaris in Anglesay. The weather grew bad and the ship was driven on to the Dutchmans's Bank, near Great Ormes Head, where she was battered by the storm and soon began to break up. The steamer was a total loss, and it is estimated that about a hundred lives were lost.

2nd 1837

This *Rothesay Castle* was an iron paddle steamer built by Tod & McGregor, 138.8 feet long, 17 feet wide, 8.6 feet in depth, and with a gross tonnage of 180. She was built for the Glasgow Castle Steam Packet Co., and was the first iron built steamer for this fleet. She had a single cylinder engine maker unknown, and during her career was reboiled in 1845. She was reputedly a very fine steamer, but her appearance is not known.

In 1849 she went to Inverness to sail in the Moray Firth. She sailed in summer only, being taken out of the water during the winter, out of danger. She sailed from Glasgow to Greenock, Dunoon, Rothesay, Tarbet, Lochgilphead and Inveraray.

Based at Inverness in 1849-50, she made occasional trips to Cromarty and did the Banavie - Inverness run. It was, however, while sailing to Loch Fyne while under charter to Messers Huchison, that the Glasgow Castle Steam Packet Co., (now operated by G. &J. Burns) decided on the first of March 1851, that she should be withdrawn and replaced by another first class steamer. In May 1851 she was sold to H.P. Maples and William Denny & Bros., who operated her between Newhaven and Dieppe. Messers Denny took over full ownership of the ship, and she was returned to the Clyde early in 1852. In 1853 while on way to take up service in Demerara she was wrecked and lost.

3rd 1854

See drawing and separate notes.

4th 1861

See drawing and separate notes.

5th 1865

Built by Henderson, Colbourn & Co., of Renfrew, for Mr A Watson and others. This steamer, as far as is known, was the last to carry the name *Rothesay Castle*. She was 203 feet long, 19.3 feet wide, had a depth of 7.9 feet, and was of 112.75 gross tons.

She was a flush decked ship with two funnels placed fore and aft the paddle boxes, a single foremast, had a steeple engine built by J. Barr & Co., and had two haystack boilers. In 1870 she was reboiled.

She started her service in 1865 on the Glasgow to Rothesay route for Mr Watson, until his death in 1866. The ship was then operated on the same route by J. Barr & Co., until she was taken over by Capt. William Buchanan in January 1874. Captain Buchanan served the Ardrossan to Arran route, and he placed the *Rothesay Castle* on this run. She stayed on this station until 1878, when she was replaced by the *Brodick Castle*.

In 1879 she was withdrawn, and in May of that year she was sold to French owners, who renamed her *Gironde Garonne*, and sailed her from Bordeaux. Her French owners sailed her until 1881, after which time she was scrapped.

ACKNOWLEDGEMENTS AND BIBLOGRAPHY

I owe my thanks to the many people in the organisations listed below for their assistance and help in obtaining the information, drawings, and pictures which made it possible for me to prepare this book.

Information sources.
The Glasgow Room, the Mitchell Library, Glasgow.
The Science & Technology Section, the Mitchell Library, Glasgow.
Glasgow University Archives and Business Records Centre.
Strathclyde Regional Archives.
The Scottish Records Office.
The Scottish Maritime Museum.
The National Maritime Museum.
Custom House, Glasgow.
Custom House, Greenock.
The Mclain Museum and Art Gallery, Greenock
The Glasgow Trarnsport Museum.
Birmingham Central Library.
Martin Bellamy BSc (Eng, Hons)

Biblography.
Scottish Classic Paddle Steamers
Alan J.S. Paterson....David and Charles, London.
First published I982.

Clyde Passenger Steamers 1812 - 1901
Capt. James Williamson....Spa Books, Ltd., Stevenage.
First published 1904.

Clyde Piers, a Pictorial Record
Ian McCrorie & Joy Montieth....Inverclyde District Llbraries, Greenock
First published 1982.

Clyde Pleasure Steamers
Ian McCrorie....Orr, Pollock & Co., Ltd., Greenock.
First published 1986.

Clyde River and Other Steamers
Duckworth & Langmuir....Brown, Son & Ferguson, Ltd., Glasgow.
First published 1937.

Clyde River Steamers of the last Fifty Years
Andrew McQueen....Gowans & Gray, Ltd., Glasgow and London.
First published 1923.

Echoes of Old Clyde Paddle Wheels
Andrew McQueen....Gowans & Gray, Ltd., Glasgow & London.
First published 1924.

Jeanie Deans
Fraser G. MacHaffie....Jeanie Deans Publications.
First published 1977.

Lochfyne
Alan Brown....Waverlay Excursions, Ltd., Glasgow.
First published 1975.

Paddle Steamers
John Woodhams....Oakfield Publications, Isle of Wight.
First published 1991.

Paddle Steamers in Camera
Allan T. Condie....Allan T, Condie Publications, Nuneaton.
First published 1987.

Passenger Steamers of the Glasgow & South Western Railway
Roy Wilson....Twelve Heads Press, Truro.
First published 1991.

Passenger Boats on Inland Waterways
D.D. Gladwin....The Oakwood Press, Dorset.
First published 1979.

Railway and other Steamers
Duckworth & Langmuir....T. Stevenson &
Sons Ltd., Lancashire.
First published 1948.

Steamboats M.K. Stammers
Shire Publications, Ltd., Aylesbury.
First published 1986.

Steamers of the Clyde
George Stromier & John Nicholson....Scottish
Field, Glasgow.
First published 1967.

Steamers of the Highands and Islands
Ian McCrorie....Orr, Pollock & Co., Ltd.,
Greenock.
First published 1987.

The Campbells of Kiklmun
Iain Hope....Aggregate Publications,
Johnstone.
First published 1981.

The Clyde
John Riddel....The Fairlie Press, Fairlie.
First published 1988.

The Clyde Passenger Steamers
Kenneth Davies....Kyle Publications, Ltd., Ayr.
First published 1980.

The Craigendorran Story
George M. Stromier....Clyde River Steamer
Club.
First published 1983.

The Denny List
David John Lyon, National Maritime
Museum.
First published 1975.

The Golden Years of Clyde Steamers
Alan J.S. Paterson....David & Charles,
London.
First published 1969.

To the Coast
Ian McCrorie....The Fairlie Press, Fairlie.
First published 1989.

Victorian Summer of Clyde Steamers
Alan J.S. Paterson....David & Charles,
London.
First published 1972.

West Coast Steamers
Duckworth & Langmuir....T. Stevenson
& Sons, Lancashire.
First published 1953.

West Highland Steamers
Duckworth & Langmuir....Brown, Son and
Ferguson, Ltd., Glasgow.
First published 1935.